The Inscrutable Shopper

The Inscrutable Shopper

Consumer Resistance in Retail

Stella Minahan

Sean Sands

Carla Ferraro

business**expert**
Press

First published in 2011 by
Business Expert Press, LLC
222 East 46th Street, New York, NY 10017
www.businessexpertpress.com

ISBN-13: 978-160649-171-3 (paperback)
ISBN-13: 978-160649-172-0 (e-book)

DOI 10.4128/9781606491720

A publication in the Business Expert Press Consumer Behavior collection

Collection ISSN: Forthcoming (print)
Collection ISSN: Forthcoming (electronic)

Cover design by Jonathan Pennell
Interior design by Scribe Inc.

First edition: August 2011

10 9 8 7 6 5 4 3 2 1

Printed in the United States of America.

Abstract

Traditional retail marketing theory has aimed to assist retailers with ideas, suggestions, and methods to attract shoppers and encourage them to spend, and ideally engender loyalty. Attracting shoppers, and encouraging them to purchase, has traditionally involved a range of marketing tactics within the retail environment, such as hanging banners, engaging barkers, playing music, designing elaborate store environments, and spending a continually increasing amount on advertising. We take a different approach with this book and ask the retailer to strategically consider and understand its customer base, particularly the issues surrounding why some customers may, or may not, choose to purchase (or shop) at all: what we define as the inscrutable shopper. While some retailers will not need to do any more than let the customer know that they exist (they have their formula just right), the reality for many retailers is that they are caught up in the business of day-to-day retail operations and lose sight of customer shifts, let alone have the time to consider why customers may not be purchasing. Hence the focus of this book is to provide an understanding of the different customer types that exist today, as a challenge of resistance to consumption. This learning is applicable to the retail industry and all stakeholders who supply it. The authors, all retail experts, have researched retail and consumer trends around the globe to develop a picture of consumer resistance in contemporary retailing, as well as provide a view of successful strategies that have been employed by other retailers to manage the inscrutable shopper. These trends, and the values and motivations that underlie them, reveal that consumer resistance can take on many forms, from a minor private concern to major public protest. The book explores the various strategies to engage inscrutable shoppers, who may be dissatisfied with ethical, green, or broader social issues. Retailers, business students, and small business owners will find the insights in this research book valuable to their efforts in being contemporary, relevant, and engaging to the often unmanageable, uncontrollable, complex, and constantly changing inscrutable shopper.

Keywords

Consumer resistance, anticonsumption, retail strategy, consumer behavior, environmentalism, green consumer, consumer boycotts

.

Contents

Introduction

Traditional marketing books provide ideas, suggestions, and methods for helping business to encourage the shopper to purchase goods and engage services. For decades, marketing and advertising gurus have exhorted retailers to hang banners, engage barkers, play music, purchase expensive store fittings, and spend more and more on advertising. This book takes a different approach and asks the retailer to think strategically about its customer base and why its customers may or may not be inclined to purchase or, even shop at all.

The information in this book, however, helps retailers and others in the supply chain to consider their current and potential customers in a way that takes into account the extremely complex environment surrounding the contemporary retailer. The framework of the book is based on an appreciation of the macro and micro forces that are contributing to—and indeed shaping—the way consumers think, which may lead them to resist consumption.

Some fortunate retailers will not need to do any more than let the customer know that they are open for business; they have the formula and customer base just right. The reality for the majority of retailers in difficult and complex times is not only to consider how to encourage the customer to purchase but also to understand why the customer is not purchasing. The focus of this book is what it means for retail when consumption falters. This is not to exclude service industries or those employed in the supply chain, such as manufacturers and distributors; the entire value chain is vulnerable to environmental turbulence and customer resistance.

This book addresses two major issues confronting retailers. The first issue is how to understand an increasingly complex and unpredictable customer who may be passively avoiding purchasing, right through to a customer participating in international boycotts of retailers. The second issue is how to respond to the customer in an increasingly turbulent business environment. The business world must now respond actively to ethical, environmental, and social issues, as well as providing relevant and appealing services.

We are asking the reader (whether a student of business, senior management at a large corporation, an owner of a small or specialist retail store, a brand owner, or marketer) to take a step back and consider how not only to encourage the customer to purchase in the first instance, but also to understand why the shopper chooses not to purchase. There is much to learn from this kind of thinking; indeed, it is an opportunity to review and reconsider what we already know in the light of the many social, political, economic, and technological changes taking place in the market.

Throughout this book, we use the term "consumer resistance" to describe the values and attributes of shoppers that led them to not buy anything, to not buy from a store, to tell their family and friends not to buy, and to organize collective actions challenging a company, brand, or even a nation. Our aims include assisting retailers and those in associated industries to understand and respond to customers that passively or actively, individually or collectively, resist consumption.

In the preparation of this book, the authors researched the global retail environment, developing economies, consumer trends, and sustainable business practices. In doing so, many senior executives across the globe were interviewed, as well as consumers. In the context of this book, the consumer research relates directly to consumer resistance by local citizens or groups, on a state or national scale.

Consumer resistance is not a static or isolated concept. It exists in a contemporary context that requires understanding, which begins with an appreciation of the complexity of the operating environment. The identification of the elements of the environment provides retailers with the opportunity to appreciate what the customer is thinking and feeling and to respond in a relevant and appropriate manner.

It is important to note that consumer resistance is not necessarily negative as it can lead to new opportunities. For example, consumer resistance to poultry farming has influenced farmers to alter their practices, leading to the availability of free-range or barn-raised poultry products. For supermarkets, these new products are an enticement for some customers to return to stores, or new customers to visit. The same can be said for fair trade coffee and numerous other production, consumption, and disposal practices.

Retail academics have for decades believed that the right merchandise at the right place, for the right price and at the right time will sell.

That holds true for most retailers, but it is only part of the story. The old mantras of merchandise may work well in many market environments and conditions, but in a turbulent environment, an inward looking focus will leave the retailer susceptible to events that can cause consumption to falter for a time at best and severely damage the business at worst. To fully understand when consumption falters, we need a better understanding of the consumer as an individual, as a member of a group, a nation, or a brand community.

Overview of the Book and Relevant Definitions

In addressing consumer resistance in retail, the book is divided into three sections: the context for consumption and the consumer society, the inscrutable shopper, and finally, the strategic retailer, which is a section on retail responses and a look at some best practice examples of what retailers can do to manage (as best as possible) the challenge of consumer resistance.

These three sections can be read sequentially or individually. There are a variety of terms used when discussing why consumers resist purchasing. We define the major terms at the end of the next section.

Part I: Retailing and the Consumer

Part I provides a history of shopping and the consumer society, current consumer values and trends, and a description of how these values and trends are shaping contemporary retailing. The importance of understanding customer resistance in retail and the need for a variety of strategic responses is also introduced.

Setting this context is important as consumer resistance emerges from social and economic history. Retail has evolved as society has developed. It has reflected and responded to the needs of the society and hence it is necessary to appreciate the development of both. In particular it is important to have some understanding of the forces that created the consumer society that is now so all encompassing. These chapters provide a brief history of modern retailing that includes looking back at how the lives of so many individuals and communities have been transformed by the shift from a society based on production to one that is largely based on consumption.

Part II: Elements of Consumer Resistance

Part II profiles shoppers and their resistant behavior. There is much evidence to demonstrate that today's customer is discerning, is value seeking, and will use multiple channels to complete the search for the right product or service. Interestingly, those same channels will also be used to decide not to purchase, to complain, or, indeed, to boycott a retailer or brand. There are many changing attributes and values that retailers need to appreciate, understand, and build into their strategic decision making.

Based on these changing attributes and values, we have developed a model of consumer resistance. It describes characteristics from macro-level values to individual shopper motivations, avoidance behaviors, and experiences. These characteristics need to be addressed by retailers looking to develop a sustainable business and maintain relevance to today's inscrutable shopper in an overcrowded marketplace.

Customer resistance is not only a multivariate phenomenon but also a dynamic one, as shoppers' preferences and the environment continue to change. Individual shoppers will respond in a variety of ways when retail offers do not meet their values and needs at the time. They may complain to their friends and others, either privately or through the use of digital and social channels, or they may become far more involved and active through the pursuit of agendas that can result in what are called "buy-cotts," which can be detrimental to any brand. The final section of part II looks at both individual and collective shopper resistance responses that are both mainstream and fringe in nature.

Part III: The Strategic Retailer

Part III concerns the retailer. In light of the uncertain and complex operating environment and the inscrutable shopper, best practice strategies are presented to assist the retailer to stay abreast and capitalize on the unpredictable nature of the inscrutable shopper and, in turn, translate lost opportunities into sales. Retailers' strategic responses are critical, and in this part we provide many examples of how retailers can meet such challenges.

A key contribution of this book is the inclusion of a section on communicating green credentials. Environmental concerns are high on the agenda for many shoppers, and the importance of communicating clearly and honestly with shoppers cannot be understated.

Scattered throughout the book are current and interesting examples of the challenges of the inscrutable shopper and the ways that leading retailers are responding.

Definitions

Before moving further into the exploration of consumer resistance, it is appropriate to distinguish between a number of terms used in such discussions. Here, we define consumer resistance, anticonsumerism, and consumerism. The aim in providing these definitions is to assist in clarifying the terminology used in this book and to assist the reader in understanding the arguments presented in the subsequent chapters.

Some of these terms are closely related in meaning. For example, terms such as "anticonsumer" can be used when discussing consumer resistance. In fact, a consumer who is displaying characteristics of resistance may be not be an anticonsumer but just cannot find what they want to purchase.

Consumer Resistance

The field of inquiry into consumer resistance is ongoing, and there have been a few research studies published in academic journals. These empirical studies cover topics from lesbian and gay pride marches,[1] Valentine's Day, alternate medical therapies,[2] the Internet,[3] and mobile phones,[4] to mobile banking[5] and biotechnologies[6] such as genetically modified foods. These studies demonstrate that consumers are able to resist consumption passively or actively. Further, shoppers are able to resist products and services, new innovations,[7] and indeed any form of change.

While not a new trend, consumer resistance has certainly seen an increasing impact on retailers in recent years. A recent study by the Australian Centre for Retail Studies showed that nearly half of all consumers would be willing to boycott retailers due to environmental concerns even if it inconvenienced them to do so. A study conducted by a research agency Consumer Sentiments showed that in 2010, 77% of consumers would boycott a company based on a poor experience while placing a complaint.[8] With the growing use of the Internet and social media sites, it is becoming increasingly easier for consumers to share their stories and encourage others to join their standpoint. For example, the Facebook group Boycott BP currently has over 800,000 members. The growing importance of understanding consumer resistance, including what drives resistance behaviors and how retailers can respond, sparked the formation of the International Centre for Anti-Consumption Research in 2005, as well as a vast array of academic research, including a special edition of the *Journal of Business Research*[9] dedicated to anticonsumption research in 2009.

The term "consumer resistance" has been in use in marketing and consumer behavior literature since the 1990s. Lisa Penazola and Linda Price developed a framework for considering consumer resistance based on dyads of the individual versus the collective, the radical versus the reformer, internal versus external, and products versus signs. The differentiation between the individual and the collective is used in this book as part of the explanation of the differing degrees of resistance that are evident in today's marketplace. In this book we use the term "resistance" to apply to consumers who exert opposition to a retail or brand offer that they regard as unacceptable.

The lack of acceptability on the part of consumers may be related to concerns about health and safety, a lack of congruence, a mismatch with their personal identity or aspirations, lack of interest in the product or retailer, convenience, speed, and value. Some examples of recent empirical studies on the antecedents of consumer resistance have focused on the country of origin, or a wish for local produce. In this context, customers may be resistant because of fears that supporting a particular retailer or product is inappropriate, as the goods are manufactured offshore and potentially are taking away local jobs. This type of nationalism is explored in more detail later in the book, as is religious fundamentalism and deep-seated brand avoidance.

In addition, the extraordinary economic changes that have occurred all around the world have resulted in the production of goods by way of automation and cheap labor. Production is no longer undertaken in the home but in conglomerates of production located where the labor is cheap and not unionized. The consumer is able to select from such a wide array of choices that it is regarded by some as being stressful for the mental health of the consumer.[10]

Customers may exert their opposition in a relatively low key way by simply avoiding certain stores or brands. Alternately, customers may become so opposed to a brand or retail offer that they become part of a collective movement that will complain, protest, or even boycott publicly.

Another form of consumer resistance emerges as a response to having an excess of material possessions. This is reflected in actions like downsizing, voluntary simplification, or regifting. Indeed, customers can become paralyzed with indecision when they confront so much choice that they do not proceed to purchase. A walk along some supermarket aisles containing vast arrays of chip and soda varieties exemplifies this "paradox of choice."[11]

Anticonsumerism

Anticonsumerism is partially a belief that material goods and possessions do not bring personal happiness and fulfillment, and can also be driven by extreme anticorporate views. It involves a range of sociopolitical consumer attitudes and activities that exist to present these alternate views. Through individual and collective action, those committed to changing the status quo in retail can exert a significant opposition. For example, anticonsumerists can directly influence the mode of consumption, from attempting to determine the price, quality, and availability of goods and services to boycotting and forming cooperatives to create an alternate provision of goods and services.

Kim Humphrey explored the positive advances of the anticonsumerism movement in his book *Excess: Anti-consumerism in the West*.[12] He interviewed activists on three continents and discusses the backlash and the varied approaches anticonsumerist activists take to inspire and promote different attitudes toward consumption. Various trends in response to Western hyperconsumption are identified, including culture jamming, downshifting, and the more recent slow-living movement as a response to the fast pace of modern life. These movements are numerous and widespread throughout the world. Consumer activism, in the form of anticonsumption, is therefore a relevant consideration for business and marketing decision making.

It is important to note that often the choices and practices of anticonsumers are centered on the search for more simplified and sustainable lifestyles and on reducing, to some degree, their personal carbon footprint and social impact. It is also important to highlight that anticonsumption is both an activity and an attitude. It is an activity of refusal, such as saying a polite "I would prefer not to buy," to holding an attitude and public stance that refuses to accept the ideology of progress and material growth.[13] These aspects are crucial to more broadly understanding consumer resistance based on a philosophy of seeking social change to the consumer society.

Globally, consumers are connecting physically and virtually and taking on corporations in a variety of ways. Such movements can be categorized into mainstream and fringe activities. Broader, mainstream activities include lifestyle movements centered on finding a more simple and sustainable lifestyle in response to the capitalist economy, including the previously discussed downshifting, voluntary simplifying, slow living, consumer boycotts, and consumer cooperatives. Fringe activities tend to be political and social movements against corporate dominance and include culture jamming, the deliberate subversion of mainstream advertising and antiglobalization, antisweatshop, antichain, and antitechnology movements that seek to prevent the adverse effects of modern technology. All these movements show the importance and relevance of anticonsumption practices in the construction of modern consumer identities.[14]

The term "anticonsumerism" is used in this book to apply to individuals who believe that happiness is not found in the acquisition of material goods; rather, they believe happiness is found in relationships with family and friends.

Consumerism

"Consumerism" can be defined as *a theory that the ever increasing production and consumption of goods and services is beneficial economically.* Consumerism is conventionally understood as referring not to the consumption of goods and services per se, but to the endless desire and routinely wasteful consumption of affluent economies.[15] There are also submovements in general that oppose consumerism in general but instead focus on green and ethical consideration, leading to customer resistance.

Before discussing the movements within the context of consumer resistance, anticonsumerism, and consumerism, it is first necessary to understand some of the history of consumer society, which is explored in the following chapter.

PART I

Retailing and the Consumer

In part I, we discuss the issue of consumer resistance in retail through three broad chapters. First, we provide an overview of the history of the consumer society, followed by a history of shopping. Setting this context is important as consumer resistance emerges from social and economic history, and given that societies and retailing have developed alongside each other, it is necessary to appreciate the development of these two interrelated areas. In these first two chapters, we present a short history of modern retailing that includes looking back at how society has been transformed as a result of the shift from a production base to a consumer society. Our final chapter in part I, chapter 3, provides a background to the types of consumers that drive resistance in retail. We provide an overview of three different (but not mutually exclusive) types of consumers: the ethical consumer, the green consumer, and the activist consumer. This context provides a foundation to move on to the broader notion of the inscrutable shopper and discuss, in greater detail, the trends, values, and motivations that drive consumer resistance in retail. In preparing this book from research conducted over the last decade, it became apparent that there are many elements of consumer resistance that are underresearched or, as of yet, not researched at all. Working within these limitations, we have identified several of these elements as areas for future research.

CHAPTER 1

A Brief History of the Consumer Society

This chapter provides some background to the significant shifts in world economies and the resultant impacts on society that have occurred over recent centuries—in particular the shift in focus from that of a production society to a pervasive consumption society, which resulted from the Industrial Revolution. In this chapter, we aim to provide background to the forces that led to the creation of the consumer society and how that changed the social fabric and community life. Here, we address three overarching issues in relation to the evolution of consumer society: the individual and consumer society, the sublimation of the individual, and the individual and self-determination. These issues underlie much of the political debates concerning the role and influence of business and commerce in contemporary society.

The era known as the Industrial Revolution (18th and 19th centuries) was a defining period for humanity. The Industrial Revolution resulted in social, political, and economic changes leading to a new society where the concerns of the individual and families shifted from day-to-day survival and in an agrarian society, to an increasingly urban and suburbanized world. Society shifted from a focus on the production of goods to a focus on the consumption of goods and services

This shift has had extraordinary repercussions in both developed and emerging economies. The desire of people for the latest, biggest, and smartest goods has grown astronomically. People no longer need to search for fuel to keep warm, to make their own clothing, to carve their own furniture, and to grow their own food. A labor force somewhere else on the planet (often in an emerging economy) produces those goods, generally at a very low cost. The goods are mass produced and then shipped to more established nations, where they are displayed in a retail store designed to entice the customer to purchase. The basis of the enticement is often not only to fulfill a need but also to create a market and to convince customers that they should need (want) the goods. Philosophers, economists, historians, and sociologists have explored the societal change in terms of both the macro social level and the impact on the individual. The following section focuses on the key concepts of production, consumption, and markets relevant to consumer resistance and retail. Readers wanting to understand the background on the consumer society can access the original works by German philosopher Karl Marx[1] and French social theorist Jean Baudrillard,[2] who wrote about the mythologies surrounding the consumer society.

Forces of globalization have had a significant impact on the shifts in capital around the world. Wealthy, developed nations are now able to purchase an ever greater variety of products and services at lower costs as the production facilities have moved to emerging economies. Often these emerging economies, historically including China and India—but also many more, sacrifice their natural environment and culture in this process. Over recent decades, consumer resistance to globalization has emerged in response to these issues.

Often the resistance is based on nationalism, religious fundamentalism, and environmentalism. These are macro-level values which can lead to consumer protest against globalization, international business entry, products' country of origin, retail formats, and trading hours. As mentioned previously, people holding nationalist, religious, and environmentalist views can express their concerns individually or as part of national or international collective cohorts.

The Individual and the Consumer Society

It is possible for individuals to be considered victims of the market and consumer society; however, they may use society to extend the quality of their lives, or in extreme cases, they may actively work to remove any market interference from their lives. According to Karl Marx[3], in subsistence societies, workers used to own their production, such as their crops. With the development of capital markets, industrialization, and mass production in factories, the workers were given wages instead of the goods that they produced. This shifted the power away from the worker. Goods were then sold into markets, often selling at a price that was out of the reach of the workers.

The Sublimation of the Individual

The consumer society developed into what theorists called consumer capitalism, consumer culture, or consumerism. Writers of the 20th century reflected on the changes and observed that the individuals are so enchanted by products and services that they are controlling their lives, providing them with new seductive material meaning.[4] The power of capital markets is such that early theorists often considered that market forces would cause all people to be enmeshed in the consumerist society and there would be no alternative to the market. As Elif Izberk-Bilgin, a professor from the University of Michigan—Dearborn, notes, despite philosophical differences, many of the major political and economic theorists over the centuries, such as Karl Marx, Max Horkeimer, Theodor W. Adorno, and Jean Baudrillard, agreed regarding the power of the individual:

> The general consensus among scholars is that the dynamics of the market economy and consumer culture would entrap all social groups equally, whether they are workers, capitalists, or intelligentsia, such that resistance to the dominance of the market is not possible.[5]

The dominance of the capitalist market over the individual was further regarded as all-embracing. Producers and marketers began to advertise and promote products by associating "consumption with freedom, democracy, civilization and success."[6]

Advertisers would present customers with manufactured goods not only as new innovations and labor saving tools, but also as emancipating and prestigious. For example, in the 1940s and 1950s, advertisers presented new appliances to women as a means to be liberated from housework and drudgery. These material goods began to take on meanings well beyond their functional value. With happiness and social status achieved (previously through family, church, or friends) but through the consumption of goods and services such as washing machines and vacuum cleaners.

Once again, in the consumer society, individuals were seen as power-less with only the option to work harder and borrow more money to achieve their goals of status via consumption. This position of perceived helplessness against the forces of the market is discussed by many authors on the topic of consumption. Opposing the view of the sublimation of the individual is the belief in individual self-determination.

The Individual and Self-Determination

The alternative to powerlessness is the concept of self-determination, where individuals are able to make real choices to achieve their goals (regardless of market forces). This idea is based on the individual rather than mass movements and is described by Elif Izberk-Bilgin as a creative movement emphasizing consumption as a means of self-expression and identity construction.[7] Individuals therefore have the ability to form their own lives within the market. In this paradigm, there are three forms of capital—economic, social, and cultural capital—all with a particular value and influence, which can be used by individuals as tools, fuel, and direction for creating a world for themselves. Under theories of self-deter-mination, for example, women can use new appliances to free themselves from time-consuming physical labor in the home.

A difficulty with this approach is that some consider the market so dominant and omnipresent that it can overwhelm any individual's actions. Along the continuum of resistance, individuals can take steps to remove themselves completely from the market in order to be free of its con-trol (known colloquially as "going off the grid" or "dropping out" into a subsistence lifestyle). There are many examples of withdrawing from the consumer society, from the extreme to the symbolic. Some individuals will attempt to not consume at all, whereas others will resist by selecting only from goods and services that meet their specific resistance criteria.

In our research, we came across examples of individuals looking to free themselves from some of the perceived burdens of consumption. For example, Jill Chivers spent a year without buying any clothes.[8] She recorded the experience in a blog:

I used to spend a lot of money on clothes. I love clothes (some of them even love me) and have a converted bedroom as a walk-in wardrobe to prove it. In 2009, my life changed but my spending didn't. I started to feel bad about what I was spending, and on December 15 of that year, I started a year without clothes shopping.

If you're fed up with bringing home 'mistake' purchases that don't really suit you, let alone will still be in style a few months from now. . . . If you sometimes hide your purchases from your partner and don't know how much you really spend on clothes, shoes, bags, accessories. . . . If you suspect that you shop to fill a need you don't quite understand . . . then help is at hand.[9]

In discussing the topic of consumer resistance with Chivers, it was clear that resistance to consumption can provide a sense of control and a freedom not available when the individual is enmeshed in the consumer society and seeking happiness through more active consumption.

However, readers of this book have been raised or spent much of their lives within a consumer society. This can make considerations of other ways of living a challenge. The history of the consumer society is not a regular discussion topic in business schools. Alternatives to the consumer society are outside the experience of most people. It is not the goal of this book to take a position on the pros and cons of the consumer society. Rather, it is our goal to highlight the changes that have occurred as a result of the rise of capital and the Industrial Revolution and may provide a background for the particular views of modern consumers and consumer groups.

The impact of the consumer society on the individual may be debated, as some consider it liberating whereas others consider it oppressive. This background on the current retail environment is important for understanding consumer resistance, whether passive or active rebellion, and whether individual or collective.

To summarize, the Industrial Revolution changed the focus of society from that of production to pervasive consumption.

To further understand consumer resistance, the next chapter is dedicated to the history of shopping. The development of retail directly reflects social change. All members of the retail industry, including customers, suppliers, manufacturers, and staff members, are entangled in consumer society. The history of shopping is a fascinating topic, as shopping has responded to social, economic, political, and technological changes, and in the future, it will likely respond to continued environmental changes. In social history, more than anything else, shopping is a story of women and how their lives have changed in the last two centuries. The next chapter looks out how the Industrial Revolution (and the resulting social changes) led to the creation of shopping facilities designed to attract women (in addition to men) to purchase.

CHAPTER 2

A Brief History of Shopping

The growth and development of the retail industry occurred alongside the processes of industrialization and urbanization of society. An understanding of the role and development of shopping provides a background as to the role of retail in modern society and sets the scene for understanding some of the reasons for consumer resistance in retail.

The retail industry began as nations industrialized and started to produce goods well in excess of their immediate requirements. At the same time, cities and suburbs were being built as people entered developed areas from rural locations in search of work. It was normal for women to be responsible for mothering and the home, whereas the father worked. As transport infrastructure improved, people, especially women, would come into town to shop.

Then in the 1880s, as town populations grew, entire suburbs were built, ringing the town with new dormitory accommodations. The town centers were the place for shops that created a female urban culture quite separate from the home. Women would travel from their suburbs, generally by train, to spend the day in the town center shopping. The sole object of the trip was to visit the growing number of shops designed and built very much with their needs in mind. The department store was a particularly successful innovation. It was an American, Gordon Selfridge (1858–1947), an entrepreneur who established a new department store in London with the female consumer in mind. He realized that shopping had become a leisure activity and a way for women to meet and socialize. As such, Selfridges department stores "offered women access to a publicly oriented social life."[1]

Gordon Selfridge believed that he satisfied women and emancipated them, providing them with a place of excitement and pleasure. He also saw shopping as being part of a "cure"—a break that would reduce women's stress and anxiety. The store not only provided the entertainment and the opportunity to be seen but also sold the clothing that would be worn at another event: "Shopping at Selfridges has all the appearance of a society gathering. It holds a recognised position on the programme of events and is responsible sartorially for much of the success of each function that takes place."[2]

Selfridges therefore offered women the opportunity to treat themselves without guilt, and for many, it became a home away from home. Yet for much of the Victorian era, shopping was regarded "as a wasteful, indulgent, immoral and disorderly pastime."[3] This disparaging and punitive judgment of women and shopping typifies the social conflict that arose as the consumer society developed. Morals and religious positions abounded to deter women from engaging with consumer goods.

By the 1900s the battle was over; women wanted to shop in the city, and did. Women could catch the train into town, have lunch, or visit the theater. Women were able to take their time browsing through the merchandise without husbands or children interrupting their thoughts. They could look at all the luxury items and enjoy them for the beautiful objects they were and not feel as though they had to purchase.

As towns grew, people began to move into the suburbs, the retailers followed, and the development of the shopping mall began. Shopping malls shifted the focus away from the department stores. The shopping malls of the 1950s and 1960s were usually long, narrow strips with an anchor (major) tenant at each end. Fortunately, more thoughtful designers quickly enhanced the bleak designs. While very few shopping centers have managed to maintain the standards of the Parisian department stores, contemporary retailers fortunately understand more about the design and service provisions in a contemporary mall.

The mall expanded the range of goods available for purchase. The anchor supermarket was supplemented with specialty stores such as apparel stores, and shoe stores, bookstores, and cafés. The goods needed for everyday survival could be purchased readily, and at the same time, the shopper could browse for discretionary items of fashion and décor:

> It may be that the future of shopping will be much more social than it is now, as customers will be looking for the kind of social interaction and experience that is difficult in an online retail environment. As it is no longer necessary to leave the house to purchase most merchandise, the social contact will become more important.

Places with great food and drink, entertainment and lots of spots for people watching will be successful.[4]

There are current signs of the decline of the mall, as the rigid designs do not provide sufficient flexibility for the customer and retailer, and there is a move back to shopping at (and supporting) local retail precincts. Further, the traditional formats surrounded by acres of parking lots are not attractive parts of the urban landscape. And for some customers, malls have become unattractive commercial spaces that alienate, rather than connect them. Malls are private commercial spaces that, for better or worse, can be seen as part of the community infrastructure, with many groups taking advantage of the facilities for exercise and social activity. There is an ongoing need for property developers to create spaces that are commercially successfully and socially acceptable to a very diverse range of shoppers. Additionally, the establishment of outlet malls has established a whole population of customers who will actively resist paying full price. We do not, however, address consumer resistance to the mall in great detail. It is very much a topic for future debate by customers, town planners, and property developers.

The history of retail is therefore, for the most part, the history of the changing circumstances of women in society. In fact, Chuihua Chung, principal of Content Design Architecture Group in New York, was clear that the history of shopping and the history of women are so tightly linked that the changes to women's lives are rapidly reflected in the development of retailing.[5]

For example, as more mothers entered the workforce, shopping malls began to extend their opening hours to allow working mothers to shop. These changes reflect the way retailers have evolved to meet the needs of women as they assumed roles outside the home. Shopping patterns also changed due to a lack of time and financial resources, with the provision of prepared frozen meals, convenience shopping formats, and one-stop-shopping lifestyle centers evidence of the busy lifestyle many women lead.[6]

The relatively recent advent of online retailing has also allowed working women to access retail services more readily. For example, the UK grocery chain Tesco is always looking to develop customer-centric strategies and recently introduced a drive-through grocery collection service. Customers order their groceries online and can then collect them via the drive-through service for a fee of £2 (US$3.30), USD which is less expensive than home delivery. The retailer believes that mothers who are balancing work and children will be attracted to this option when compared to the struggle of supermarket shopping with kids in tow.[7]

Early collective resistance to retailers began with the establishment of consumer groups. According to Carol McPhee and Ann Fitzgerald,[8] authors of *The Non-Violent Militant: Selected Writings of Teresa Billington-Grieg*, groups led by the suffragette activist Teresa Billington-Grieg consisted of working-class women. The makeup of the groups changed over time, and by the 1950s the consumer groups became more gender neutral. Australian consumer advocate magazine Choice has been one of the more vocal consumer groups in the global retail landscape. Independent and transparent, Choice was founded in 1960 to ensure the consumer voice is heard, and the organization is always on the hunt for misleading retail practices, assisting consumers through changes to laws and industry behavior.[9]

The history and development of retail has focused mainly on women, and this focus has, in part, been to the exclusion of men. Thomas Hine found that men rank shopping as one of their least favorite leisure activities.[10] Men do not feel as though they are achieving anything through shopping. The underlying notion here is that men have a different set of priorities, preferences, and attitudes that result in different gender responses, decision processes, and purchase outcomes.[11]

Men are not taught to shop, and by and large do not enjoy the processes of shopping pursued by many women as recreation. Specialty stores such as Home Depot and Cabela's are naturally more attractive to men because they offer a range of goods that they may seek, such as technical and electronic goods, as well as hobby items for hunting, fishing, and shooting. Research conducted by Stella Minahan in 2003 and 2004 in South Africa, Australia, and the United Kingdom demonstrated that there is a generation gap among men in relation to shopping. In this research, younger men report shopping as a leisure activity compared with older men who tended to see shopping as almost exclusively "women's work" and something that has to be tolerated and rationalized.[12]

It is important to acknowledge that consumer resistance is a difficult topic to come to terms with, as the majority of Americans and citizens of wealthy countries have been born and raised in a culture where consumption is a large part of the way we define ourselves and others. The reality remains that consumer society is the dominant force in our lives. Juliet Schor undertook research that attempts to delve into the nature of consumerism and its impact on society.[13] She argues that anticon-sumerism holds attention most at an individual level, and that there is very little "critical politics of consumption." There is little debate from either side of politics of the role and impact of consumption on the average American. The individual continues to regard shopping as an essential part of her life and leisure, spending many hours and days at malls both during the work week and on holidays. The traffic headed for the many outlet malls in the United States on holidays is confirma-tion of Schor's assertion. Yet, she reports, the average American remains concerned about their quality of life and whether the attention to shop-ping, specials, discounts, coupons, and new merchandise is actually an improvement to life. The concern is that consumers rarely act on this, and, as Schor argues, there are few mechanisms in place to encourage this and for average Americans to act on their concerns for the quality of their lives.

According to Schor, we no longer seek to keep up with the "Joneses."[14] Our aspirations have risen steadily to the point where it is no longer enough to have material equality with one's neighbors. We now seek to emulate the celebrities in Hollywood and the lifestyles of the rich and famous. This desire to consume places significant stresses on the family unit. Seeking this life leads to indebtedness and bankruptcies for many. Two incomes are needed to provide all the essentials of contemporary life; home theaters with the associated equipment, personal computers, mobile phones for all members of the household, and regular upgrad-ing of the domestic décor have become the norm. Schor argues that this pursuit does not bring happiness; the reverse is in fact true with family breakdowns resulting from the stress of seeking more and more goods. As such, she proposes an alternative view based on personal choice and discretion. The following are her propositions:

- The consumer is rational and will act to her or his own well-being.
- The consumer is informed about the product offerings in the marketplace.
- Consumer preferences are consistent over time.
- Every consumer has preferences that are independent of other consumers' preferences.

- The production and consumption of goods have no external effects.
- There are complete and competitive markets that are alternatives to consumption.

Much of Schor's thesis relates to the act of shopping. For example, the shopper is normally concerned with getting the best value for the product that she or he has already decided to purchase. While this is true for some shoppers, it certainly does not hold true for those who impulse buy, for those who do not have enough time to do the necessary information gathering, for those who elect not to spend the time gathering information, or for those for whom the whole process of shopping is disliked. Schor presents a way of looking at consumption that maintains the concept of rational behavior. However, this position is rarely supported in a postmodern world.

Consumers are not always rational, and their preferences change constantly over time. A number of factors impact this change and associated consumer choices; some consumers are more motivated to comparison shop for the best prices, whereas others are more convenience oriented. Some consumers may be brand loyal and some may be impacted by various marketing efforts, such as celebrity endorsements. Personality also impacts retail decisions, as some may find shopping a bore and some consider shopping a favorite leisure activity. Consumers only tend to change their behavior through learning. For example, they will avoid restaurants they have found to be crowded and will settle on brands that best meet their tastes. The message is clear: consumers are not stagnant beings: They change as they age, as society changes and each generation will present retailers with new challenges. The key to keeping ahead of the changing consumer curve is to remain focused on product and service segmentation and to ensure that the customer is always at the center of the product or service's design. This reinforces the notion of the inscrutable shopper (introduced in the following chapter, and discussed at length throughout this book), who is not only difficult to define but also nearly impossible to predict.

We contend that resistance to consumption has grown over time in response to perceived inequities and failure of service.

The next chapter outlines three key segments relevant to consumer resistance in retail: the ethical consumer, the green consumer, and the activist consumer.

CHAPTER 3

The Inscrutable Shopper

In this chapter we discuss three consumer types as identified in our primary and secondary research. They are the ethical consumer, the green consumer, and the activist consumer, each of whom has gained a high profile in society and have an impact on the retail industry. The evidence for these segments is based on many financial and economic indicators of the growing success of products that are ethically and environmentally sound. The chapter also presents the results of research into consumer perceptions of retail brands in this regard and how retailers have responded to calls for transparent ethical and green compliance throughout the supply chain. As mentioned earlier, we seek to provide an understanding of those elements of consumer resistance most relevant to retailers. In chapter 4 we undertake a much more detailed look at the forces of consumer resistance.

Modern consumer society is fragmented, and postmodern consumer theory[1] suggests that the quickened pace of postmodern life engenders a condition of hyperreality in which the real becomes not only that which can be reproduced but that which is already reproduced: the hyperreal.[2] In postmodern society, the individual's authentic self is splintered and displaced by a made-up self,"[3] and as Professor Yiannis Gabriel, or Royal Holloway University of London, and Professor Tim Lang, of City University London[4] point out, consumers can adopt one of many "faces" corresponding to certain social roles in which the consumer is empowered. In their book *The Unmanageable Consumer*, Gabriel and Lang synthesize different academic, social, and political discourses on different representations of consumption and customers. They present a number of distinctive portraits of the customer—chooser, communicator, explorer, hedonist, and discuss the paradigms and perspectives underpinning these images. Gabriel and Lang contend that none of these different customer portraits satisfactorily comes to terms with the fragmentation, volatility, and confusion of contemporary consumption.

And hence the concept of the inscrutable shopper is introduced here to capture the defiance of today's consumerism. Three of the faces relevant to retail and consumer resistance (Gabriel and Lang identify nine such faces) are the consumer as citizen, the consumer as rebel, and the consumer as activist. Importantly, the authors note that consumer culture has become a way to differentiate one's self by constructing unique identities without fear of reproach from the binding influence of social bonds and moral obligations. Within each of these different faces, consumers can occupy many different spaces in terms of resistance—we focus on the ethical, the green, and the activist consumer as a resistant consumer typology.

The Ethical Consumer

Ethical, or socially conscious, consumers intentionally purchase products and services made by companies that operate in an ethical manner. Alternatively, they might choose to not purchase or to consume in a minimalist manner. A stance on ethical consumerism may mean consumption with minimal harm to or exploitation of humans, animals, and the natural environment. Ethical consumers behave accordingly by way of simple practices, such as positive buying, which involves favoring ethical products such as fair trade, cruelty free, organic, recycled, reused, or produced locally, or take more complex stances such as boycotting goods produced by child labor.[5] To assist with the identification of these products, a number of standards and labels have been introduced around the world, such as fair trade, Organic Trade Association certified, union made, Rainforest Alliance certified, dolphin safe, and free range.

Ethical goods and services are experiencing growing market shares around the world, and consumers are becoming more aware of ethical consumption through market and information campaigns.[6]

In the UK over the last two years, expenditure on ethical food and drink increased 27 per cent to reach £6.5 billion, representing eight per cent of all food and drink sales. Fairtrade food grew by 64 per cent to reach £749 million, while sales of animal welfare Freedom Food certified products tripled in two years to reach £122m. Sales of organic food fell by 14 per cent to £1,704 million.[7]

Growth has remained positive during the 2 years of the recession and is particularly prominent in the fast-moving consumer goods sector. A survey by leading market research firm IGD uncovered that 30% of shoppers in Germany, 29% in the United Kingdom, 24% in France, and 9% in Spain actively consider two or more ethical factors when making purchases.[8]

Ethical consumers are highly principled and aware, with many boycotting real animal-fur products or products that involve the use of animals in product testing.[9] They also examine a company's record on hiring and promoting minorities and women.[10] Ethical consumers care whether a corporation promotes employees from minority ethnicities, and plan personal consumption to avoid harm to animals. They are concerned about product transportation distances, such as food miles, as well as a plethora of related concerns.

Direct consumer action in the form of boycott activity, pressure groups, and other forms of consumer activism is also on the rise. Hence it may well be that consumer values are experiencing a shift from the inward facing materialistic outlook, often associated with the "yuppie" mind-set of the 1980s, toward a more outward focused, socially and environmentally proactive mind-set. The American and European consumer, in particular, is becoming increasingly concerned with social responsibility, as reflected in shifting consumer values.

Market research group *GfK NOP* conducted a five-country (Germany, the United States, Britain, France, and Spain) study of consumer beliefs about the ethics of large companies. The report is described in a *Financial Times* article published in February 2007 titled "Ethical Consumption Makes Mark on Branding" and was followed up by an online discussion.[11] More than half of respondents in Germany and the United States believed there is a serious deterioration in the standards of corporate practice. Almost half of those surveyed in Britain, France, and Spain held similar beliefs. About a third of respondents said they would pay higher prices for ethical brands. The most ethically perceived brands were The Co-op (United Kingdom), Coca-Cola (United States), Danone (France), Adidas (Germany), and Nestlé (Spain). Interestingly, Coca-Cola, Danone, Adidas, and Nestlé did not appear in the United Kingdom's list of the 15 most ethical companies and Nike appeared in the lists of the other four countries, but not in the United Kingdom. In 2011, Westpac, the National Australia Bank and the ANZ Bank were named three of the five world's most ethical banks. Some of the best-known U.S. companies listed for 2011 included retailers Whole Food Market, Best Buy and Target as well as online retailer Zappos and auction site eBay, made the Ethisphere Institute's 2011[12] ranking of the 100 most ethical companies.

It is clear that the ethical consumer is concerned not only with the product, but also with the companies that manufacture, distribute, and sell them.

The rising popularity of organic and fair-trade products can be largely attributed to the ethical consumer. The U.S. Organic Trade Association released findings from its 2010 Organic Industry Survey, highlighting that organic product sales in 2009 grew by 5.3% to reach US$26.6 billion (US$24.8 billion representing organic food alone).[13] Conversely, UK sales have decreased in the period from 2008 to 2009, with sales dropping from £2.1 billion in 2008 to £1.84 billion in 2009.[14] Although Asia has been slow to adopt the organic trend, over the past several years, countries like Japan, Singapore, Malaysia, Korea, and Taiwan have seen annual growth in demand of 20% to 30%, as noted by Jo Cadilhon of the Food and Agriculture Organization of the United Nations (UN).[15] However, a growing minority of urban consumers in emerging Asian countries is starting to develop in countries like the Philippines, Thailand, India, China, and Malaysia.

As is the case for environmentally friendly products, the organic sector is showing strong patterns of sustained growth during difficult economic times and is in line with the increasing number of consumers educated about their food choices. The demand for organic food and drinks is proving to be resilient in a number of key markets and product sectors, due to a combination of key factors. First, regular purchasers of organics typically have significantly higher than average disposable incomes and have so far been largely unaffected by the current global downturn. Second, the price differential between many organic and regular products has contracted steadily in recent years, and this has increased consumer reluctance to revert to cheaper, nonorganic alternatives.

Sales of fair-trade-certified products have also been growing rapidly, with consumers around the world spending around US$5.4 billion on fair-trade products in 2009, a 15% increase over 2008.[16] Further, almost 27,000 fair-trade-certified products are now sold in more than 70 countries. Combined, the Australian and New Zealand markets were one of the top three for growth in sales of fair-trade products in 2009, with an increase of 58%, just behind Canada at 66% and Finland at 60%. Strong growth was also recorded in established fair-trade nations such as the United Kingdom, where growth hit 14%, and the United States, where sales increased 7%. Fair-trade products also gained new customers outside of its traditional markets, and sales grew exponentially in Eastern Europe, South Africa, and many other countries in the global south.[17]

It is important to note, however, that despite growing interest in fair trade offerings, only a minority of shoppers is routinely buying such products. Datamonitor 2010[18] research found that while the vast majority of consumers believe it is important to choose grocery products that support fair trade, only 23% are buying such products regularly (i.e., most of the time or all the time) on a global scale.

The Green Consumer

Green consumerism is a concept generally accepted as emerging from Environmentalism and is linked to ethical consumerism. The distinction between green consumerism and ethical consumerism is important because ethical concerns encompass a broader set of social issues and therefore involve a more complex decision-making process. The definition of the ethical consumer movement encompasses issues associated with purchase behavior, including animal welfare and fair-trade, labor standards, and health concerns addressed by organic food. Ethical consumers are additionally concerned with the people element of consumerism, being "distinguished by their concern for deep seated problems, such as those of the Third World."[21]

In the context of this book, we define the green consumer as primarily and consistently focused on environmental issues.

The surge in environmentalism has resulted in a new niche market of consumers. These consumers might choose to consume less in their daily lives, or they may at times even spend more to be environmentally responsible. Lifestyles of health and sustainability (LOHAS) is commonly used to refer to this consumer group. The LOHAS market is substantial and is growing at more than 20% annually.[22] This growing market has a worth in excess of US$550 billion annually and, according to the Natural Marketing Institute (NMI),[23] 19% of the U.S. population, or 40 million consumers, regularly purchase eco-friendly products and play an active and loyal role in protecting the environment. In comparison, 15% of the UK population has adopted a LOHAS lifestyle. In 2008, U.S. consumers spent almost US$300 billion on LOHAS-related products and services. In Australia, the LOHAS market is conservatively estimated to be worth US$31 billion by end 2012.[24] Recent research by the NMI of over 50,000 consumers in over 20 countries found that approximately two-thirds of consumers care about the environment, but their purchases are primarily determined by price, and 8 in 10 consumers are interested in some type of green product.[25]

LOHAS-aligned consumers display many different consumption behaviors, such as taking sustainability into account when choosing a brand, seeking out green products or products with eco-friendly packaging, considering fair trade or environmental practices when choosing where to shop, and buying organic products. But who are these people? What drives them to consume less and be green? For business to capitalize on this market segment, it is important to understand who these people are, what shapes their consumption choices, and in turn how business can assist them in their environmentally conscious consumption.

These consumers are hard to define. Being green extends throughout the population to varying degrees, and green concerns are extremely diverse, encompassing a wide range of issues. However, a number of studies have identified some commonalities among these consumers. For instance, younger individuals tend to be more sensitive to environmental issues, as they have grown up in a period in which such concerns were more salient than in the past. However, this does not mean that these consumers are exclusively young. Baby boomers are also actively following this movement and tend to be influenced by their children, as they have both the time to seek out specialty items and the resources to afford premium-priced products. ICOM Information & Communications,[26] a Toronto-based target-marketing company, surveyed over 6,000 women in the baby boomer demographic. The study found that these women are more likely to use green products. In fact, women in their thirties and forties with one (or more) children living at home are a key target market. People in higher social classes and income brackets are more likely to be aware of, and to purchase, environmentally friendly products.

Green consumers also vary in terms of their personalities, values, attitudes, interests, and lifestyles—variables referred to in market research as psychographic variables. Johanna Moisander and Sinikka Pesonen,[27] of the Helsinki School of Economics, conceptualize green consumerism as a personal ethical orientation or as a set of proenvironmental personal values and attitudes that inform a particular form of socially conscious or socially responsible decision making. Green consumers tend to be goal-oriented individuals who take into account the environmental consequences (in terms of costs and benefits) of their private consumption in an attempt to reduce their personal impact on the environment. They also tend to have more liberal beliefs and are more likely to exhibit strong environmental commitment than those with more conservative political views. The values of green consumers are multifaceted and encompass beliefs about the environmental impact of the materials and processes used to manufacture products and their packaging; the methods of product distribution, sale, and disposal; and the company's corporate philosophy and reputation for environmental stewardship.

Discussions have emerged in recent times as to whether the Green Movement is a fad destined to decline during downturns in the economy. The most recent decline in economies globally curtailed consumer spending in virtually every product category; however, a steady stream of research supported the argument that consumers were still environmentally conscious during this time. They were still demanding that the brands they interacted with were environmentally and socially responsible. According to Havas Media, part of the Havas worldwide communications group,[28] 79% of consumers still preferred to buy products from environmentally responsible companies in 2009. These figures are supported conducted by custom market research firm, Harris Interactive that showed that 73% of U.S. consumers were still buying green despite the tough economic times. In fact, they found 26% of U.S. consumers were buying more green products and services. Interestingly, these environmentally conscious consumers are also in emerging markets such as China and India, with nearly half willing to pay a 10% premium for products produced in an environmentally and socially responsible way.

However, a 2009 national survey by public relations firm the Shelton Group[30] in the United States revealed that the recession has altered the underlying motivations for consumers purchasing in a green and sustainable manner. Whereas in 2006 the top reason was protecting the environment, in 2009 the top reason cited was saving money. This shift

in underlying motivations points to one of the elements of the inscrutable shopper: conflict. There are many situations in which the ethical and
green consumer feels compromised and conflicted when the values he or
she holds are in opposition.[31] As reported by the Shelton group, there is
still resistance to paying more for goods that are seen as green when personal finances are stretched, which occurs in economic downturns.

The Activist Consumer

The third group of shoppers we discuss is the activist, or those shoppers that actively resist consumption. These customers can often seek
out others and organize themselves into groups that actively campaign
in a variety of ways in attempt to influence a company or other shoppers to join in active rebellion. A common form of resistance is customer
boycotts. Boycotts have become more potent in recent decades with the
development of global telecommunications facilities and social network-
ing software, and e-mail allowing for rapid and global messaging.

Activist consumers' influence can be thought to be the greatest in
industries where products are not well differentiated and where competition is intense. Activism concerning the environment is commonly used
by many environmental non-governmental organizations. For example,
activism has occurred toward cosmetic firms (e.g., Procter & Gamble and
Colgate-Palmolive) because of their use of animal testing and major oil
companies (e.g., British Petroleum, Esso, and Shell) for their environmental damages and their supposed lobbying efforts to deter climate-change
policies. Some large fast-food companies (e.g., McDonald's) are targeted
by boycott campaigns because of their supposed unethical meat-produc-
tion practices. Finally, some non-governmental organizations support the
boycott of non-certified tropical timber to protest against unsustainable
harvest practices. The objective, therefore, is to put enough pressure on
the target to encourage it to change its behavior.

Australian academic Helene Cherrier conducted a study on anticonsumption discourses and customer resistant identities.[32] She interviewed
culture jammers to attain first-person descriptions of their everyday experience with customer resistance. "Culture jamming" is the term given to
organized social activism that attempts to reduce the impact of consumption messages in the mass media. An entertaining example of culture

THE INSCRUTABLE SHOPPER   31

jamming is displayed by the U.S.-based comic actor "Reverend Billy and his Church of Life After Shopping."[33] Reverend Billy is the stage name of the actor who uses theater in shopping malls and stores, on the street, and on current affairs programs to highlight "the evils of consumption." His activism has enjoyed a high profile, but it is not yet clear whether his efforts have raised interest in anticonsumption, highlighted existing levels of interest, or adversely raised the profile of certain retail stores.[34] The performances are highly engaging and entertaining, as described by one audience member:

> Their message is clear and direct: Stop shopping! Break your addiction! Resist that product! Reduce your consumption! Throw away your credit cards! Liberate yourself from debt! Walmart, Starbucks, Disney, and the other big retail corporations are destroying local neighborhoods as well as the planet. Their products are based on slave labor. Their employees are paid peanuts. Stop buying, start loving! We don't need products to mediate love! Change-a-lu-ya! Welcome to the Church of Stop Shopping![35]

Consumer activism can be public, organized, and mainstream or fringe and theatrical (as with the case of Reverend Billy).

Part I Summary

Part I has set the scene for a discussion of consumer resistance in retail by discussing three major areas impacting resistance behavior in modern society. Shifts in world economies, new technologies and political structures, and the resultant impact on society that have occurred over recent centuries have led to the creation of the consumer society. This, in turn, has created shifts in the social fabric and community life. Alongside this change, and the processes of industrialization and urbanization, the growth and early development of the retail industry occurred. Today, shopping forms part of the fabric that ties modern society together (for better or worse). Given many of the downstream effects of retail (i.e., on manufacturing and living conditions in the Third World), recent times have seen a rise of consumer resistance. Further, the consumer's search for identity and meaning, within a fragmented society, has resulted in some consumers adopting one of the many faces of consumption. This has led to different types of resistance, which are important for retailers to consider: the ethical consumer, the green consumer, and the activist consumer. This context provides the base to move on to the broader notion of resistance and provides a foundation for the development of a model of consumer resistance, allowing a deeper understanding of why and how consumer resistance is manifest in retail.

PART II

Consumer Resistance

In the retail industry, trends (or changes in patterns of behavior) are most commonly set by consumers, and the marketplace follows. In the past, these trends changed slowly, providing retailers with the opportunity to analyze their implications and make well-informed decisions. Recently, these trend cycles have been emerging more rapidly as a result of technology, accelerated social diffusion, instantaneous communication, and an increased willingness to accept (or inability to escape) new ideas.[1] The changing nature of consumer trends means that retailers need to become more observant and better prepared when making strategic decisions. With this in mind, consumer resistance is an important topic for retailers to consider. In modern times, resistance in retail is not solely an act of individual or collective protest. In times gone by, the most common images of consumer resistance may have been protesters targeting large corporations for their manufacturing, wage, or human rights negligence. Today, consumer resistance includes a wide range of individual and collective behaviors, many of which can occur in private. For instance, a consumer might drop out of consumption by deciding not to buy certain products for a range of reasons.

In part II of the book, we set out to examine consumer resistance in the context of retail and, to this end, we have two objectives. First, we propose a model of consumer resistance in retail. This is important in order to frame the context in which consumers are operating, or the forces that exist that lead consumers to decide to be resistant. To assist in understanding why a customer may become resistant to consumption or the retail offer, it is important that we develop a picture of the macro and micro trends and drivers that are influencing the inscrutable shopper and leading to resistant responses to the retail offer.

CHAPTER 4

A Model of Consumer Resistance

We present a model of shopper resistance to assist with a better understanding of the underlying drivers. The model is developed from the current state of the retail environment, the general state of sociopolitical turbulence evident in the global economy, and the changing nature of the shopper. Customer trends and needs largely define the context within which retail organizations function and, as such, are key drivers of the market economy. The degree of confidence customers have in their ability to spend and manage debt can have a significant effect on overall demand and, in turn, on economic growth, job creation, and investment. In this context, customer change is represented by trends, which are influenced by social, political, economical, and cultural factors, as well as movements in demographics. The aim of our model is to provide the reader with a visual reference to the main attributes of consumer resistance, from macro to micro drivers and related customer responses. In terms of responses, the model encapsulates the shopper as being either passively or actively resistant, owing largely to an imbalance in the matching of their requirements with the retail offer.

Our model presents five broad elements in consumer resistance:

1. Macro-level values and trends in society
2. Internal motivations driving the individual
3. Internal experience of the individual
4. Conflict
5. Consumer responses

The factors are elaborated on in Table 4.1 and visually presented in our model (Figure 4.1). With the first factor, the model takes account of

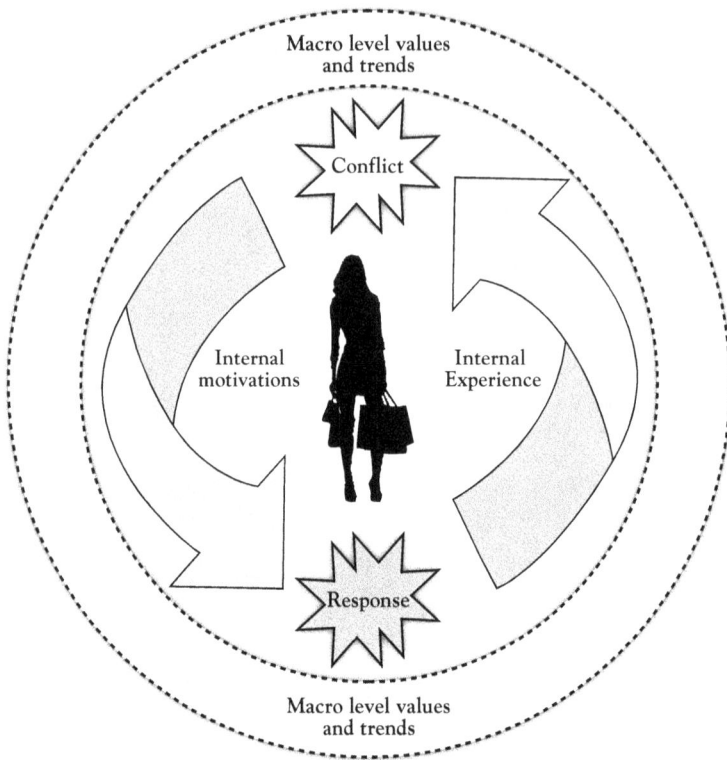

Figure 4.1. Individual dissonance leading to consumer resistance.

the macro-level values of nationalism, religious fundamentalism, brand activism, and environmentalism, plus macro-level trends of nostalgia, cocooning, increased physical mobility (both cultural and social), and the search for community. The building of the model continues to the second and third factors: internal motivations and internal experience. We propose that a consumer's internal motivations and internal experience are interlinked, in that when there is conflict between consumers' internal motivation and their experience, there is a reaction, a possible conflict, and in extreme cases, consumer resistance. The model is particularly useful in that it is combined with that developed by associate professor Susan Fournier of Boston University,[2] which demonstrates the dynamic nature of customers in terms of their mainstream resistant behaviors (encompassing avoidance, minimizing behaviors, and rebellion) and is extended to include fringe responses (all the behaviors detailed in Table 4.1).

Table 4.1. Elements of Consumer Resistance

	Factors Leading to Possible Conflict		Response	
1. Macro-Level Trends and Values	2. Internal Motivations	3. Internal Experience	4. Mainstream	5. Fringe
Nostalgia	Economic value	Boredom	Avoidance	Antiadvertising
Cocooning	Health	Cynicism	Minimization	Antiwaste
Mobility	Convenience	Too much choice	Rebellion	Antiglobalization
Community	Identity creation			Antisweatshop
Nationalism	Security, safety, and risk aversion			Anti–chain store
Religious Fundamentalism	Empowerment through collectives			Antitechnology
Environmentalism				

The elements identified in Table 4.1 are macro-level trends and values that, combined with internal motivations and experiences, can lead either to a satisfactory retail experience or, if the elements are in conflict and are not aligned to the needs of the customer, to a conflict and possibly a response. This response may be a mainstream or fringe form of consumer resistance.

Macro-level Values and Trends

The first part of our model captures the macro-level values and trends that surround consumers today. As discussed in chapter 1, the Industrial Revolution led to challenges to the social order, with a focus on consumption rather than production that has led to the all-embracing consumer society. Several macro trends are influencing current retail consumption, such as nostalgia, cocooning, mobility, and the desire for community. Each of these macro-level trends and drivers is discussed in more detail in the next sections. Three other macro-level values that have emerged within the new world order are nationalism, religious fundamental-ism,[3] and environmentalism. These values are complex and are deeply embedded in the individual and collective psyche. In relation to the retail industry and consumer behavior, both nationalism and religious funda-mentalism are underresearched areas of focus. This chapter introduces these topics briefly and notes the need for further research.

Nostalgia

In response to the stresses of a continually changing society, growing economic uncertainty, and the prevalence and dominance of technol-ogy, shoppers are reaching back toward "long-gone better days." Much of the appeal of historical revivalism and nostalgia stems from our increasingly turbulent society; customers are desperately longing for simpler days, unburdened by the war on terror, Internet scandals, and climate change. In the context of retailing, nostalgia can be defined as a market preference for products and images that were popular in the past but can no longer be easily sourced. The trend of nostalgia also reflects customers' desire to empower their lives by reconnecting with their idealized and more peaceful past. In uncertain times, peo-ple retreat into fantasies of childhood or the illusions good old days. Importantly, nostalgia is not simply about reliving the past; it is also about reinterpreting it, and this is particularly true for younger cus-tomers. While younger customers have adopted many products and fashions from the past as their own, they often update or reinvent them. In this instance, nostalgia has little to do with longing for an era they never experienced—it is about rediscovery.

Nostalgia is seeping into nearly every aspect of customer culture, which is also playing into acts of resistance to new and novel goods and ways of doing business. For example, there is a resurgence in interest from young females in the craft of knitting. Groups have been established all over the globe as opportunities to meet and share the do-it-yourself (DIY) craft that has not been actively practiced since the 1960s. It was around this decade that the cost of commercially produced yarns and knitted goods became mass produced with an associated dramatic reduction in costs. The cost of the yarn, the skills required, plus the hours of effort meant that it was no longer attractive for women to knit. It was much easier, quicker, and cheaper to go to the local department store and chose from a wide range of affordable knitwear. It was not until the 1990s that the revival in knitting began to be evident, reaching a peak in the early part of this century.

Knitting groups, similar to that of quilting circles, are normally conducted away from public view, despite the efforts of many knitters to come out during the 1990s and early 2000s when they would meet in public places such as hotels and cafés to practice their crafts and socialize.[4] Apart from creating the traditional baby apparel, there has been evidence of a strong reinterpretation of the past, such as knitting protective covers for iPads and other electronic devices. Such efforts are effective in that that they look so incongruous and are representative of nostalgia, cocooning, and warmth, as well as rebellion.

The need to recall the past is associated with a growing demand for vintage products and brands. This trend is affecting everything from cars to confectionary but is particularly evident in categories such as clothing and footwear, homewares, and toys. As a result, fashion catwalks and retail outlets continue to feature vintage-inspired clothing and accessories; there is a growing demand for household furniture and appliances from the 1950s, 1960s, and 1970s; and revived sales for retro toys such as Cabbage Patch Kids, My Little Pony, Care Bears, and Raggedy Ann dolls. A look at supermarket shelves also reflects the nostalgia trend with packaged goods appearing as though they are from another era, and old advertisements are being recycled to appeal to wistful customers.

Cocooning

In the current economic state, consumer behavior is similar to that of past recessions, where a shifting consumer attitude was seen and consumers were more careful in their spending and were cocooning.[5] The term "cocooning" was coined during the 1991 recession and characterizes the shift to consumers creating passive home life environments, retreating and spending more leisure time in the home. The difference between the passive act of cocooning during the 1991 recession and today, is that is consumers still want to remain connected, using the home as a retreat, but staying connected to the outside world using online and e-commerce sources to build stronger social networks and family connections.[6] As described in this quote from one business woman,

> One of the things that I've noticed more and more is that people will BlackBerry me in the evening, you know, after 8:30 in the evening. I'm pretty much settled in and people know that it [BlackBerry] sits next to me, my cup of tea is there, my knitting is in my lap, something's on television and I just take care of business. "Linda, do you think you can order this, this and this for me?" Fine. Sure.[7]

The importance of this image is that it is not of the late night stay at the office but in her lounge with her knitting and a cup of tea. She is choosing to work from the cocoon of her home. This image is one that is becoming more and more familiar as the traditional nine-to-five work format declines and more geographically and temporal flexibility enters working agreements.

Mobility

Shoppers are also increasingly more mobile than they were decades ago. This increase in mobility has been driven by four major factors.[8] The first is *social mobility*, which refers not only to an increased standard of living, but also to an increasing desire to demonstrate it publicly. Second is a form of *physical mobility*, driven through the growth of low-cost air travel, resulting in more people experiencing more of the world. Third is a *virtual mobility*, where there is a growing importance of mobile technology in people's lives, bringing them closer together, regardless of physical distance. Fourth is *cultural mobility*, referring to consumers becoming more open to foreign ideas, be that cuisine (e.g., tapas), pop culture (e.g., Sudoku), or brands (e.g., beer). Consumers are increasingly aware of different cultures, products, brands, and so on, which has a very real impact on their requirements and expectations for their local retail environment. This was echoed in our interviews, as is demonstrated in the following quote:

> The other thing is choice [has increased]. . . . As travel has increased, people have broadened their repertoires. When you look at what people eat, they belong to a much wider church . . . and that breadth of choice has reflected on retail significantly. And it brings its own side as to how best to manage choice and range.

The development of enhanced levels of social, physical, virtual, and cultural mobility directly contributes to the increase in the complexity of the shopper environment.

Community

Consumers are increasingly seeking to be part of a community, real or virtual. New social media are empowering both the retailer and the individual to participate in the broader community. Take the knitting circle movement for example, a form of collective leisure and a means of building connection, community, and social capital while remedying the individualism typical of the present information society,[9] and the possibility of nostalgia through a romantic return to simpler times or to an idealized past.[10] While the knitting movement has not the celebrity it once had in the popular press, it appears that young females are still turning to knitting as the Knitting Guild of America has reported a 21% growth in its membership since 2001.[11] At the same time, there has been an extraordinary growth in blog forums that are based around the topic of knitting.[12]

This desire for community is driving consumer review content, a process whereby consumers exchange information on products, brands, and services, with most of this exchange now taking place via online channels. By establishing this online communication, retailers can then collect, monitor, and participate in these discussions and can get up-to-date feedback; even testing product ideas can be achieved through the online channel. Some retailers and manufacturers have considered how they may engage communities of interests with their products and services. For instance, diaper manufacturer Huggies set up a new community with advice and information at HuggiesBabyNetwork.com. The online presence aims to grab mothers' attention when they first discover they are pregnant and retain their loyalty during the newborn, infant, and toddler phases. Features include expert advice, a virtual nursery creator, an online community, and of course, Huggies product information. Microblogging website Twitter is currently developing a variety of tools for use by companies and brands to offer an up-to-date account of the current discussions among its members. Luxury fashion brand Louis Vuitton was among one of the first brands to take advantage of social network advertising, promoting their website and new product offerings through Twitter.[13] Meanwhile, Facebook has also proven to be a powerful and convenient way to reach customers, enabling companies to post photos, videos, or status updates and even collect consumer feedback and opinions. With more than 500 million active users worldwide, Facebook earned roughly US$500 million in net profit in 2010.[14] In recognition of this significant reach, Starbucks used Facebook to find almost 1.5 million friends to raise awareness of their brand while raising money for AIDS, which became the most viral event in Facebook history.

The major macro-level trends of nostalgia and cocooning, increased mobility, and need for connection with the local community are clear at all levels of society in major economies around the world. These trends are important, and in many cases, have been identified by retailers who are in tune with the customer. These macro-level trends provide an important background to the underlying drivers of consumer resistance.

Nationalism

In this era, collective consumer resistance based on nationalism is expressed in a variety of ways around the globe.

Nationalism in retail is often expressed through country-of-origin debates,[15] but there has been little empirical research relating to retail in the last decade. Country of origin is still believed to have an impact on consumer choice, but how much is related to nationalism is not known. In the past, country of origin has become so important to consumers that labeling of goods in this way was introduced. Other forms of nationalist fervor has been expressed commercially in advertising campaigns that encouraged consumers to support local industries by purchasing goods manufactured locally, such as the Buy Australian campaigns of the 1980s. These campaigns are not as prevalent now that most manufacturing has globalized, and it is extremely difficult for a multisite, multibrand retailer to provide only locally sourced goods. However, the cohort of customers who want to purchase locally produced goods and services remains a powerful force in the marketplace.

There are groups of workers and consumers from the richer nations who are concerned about job losses resulting from the shift of production to poorer nations. They want to see the production jobs stay in their own country and the goods produced to be sold in their own country, as well as exported for sale. This nationalism struggles in the face of the lower cost structures resulting from global manufacturing efforts.

Other examples of nationalism occur in emerging economies with religious beliefs driving the active protests against retail development. In India, Hindu nationalism has emerged as a concern for retailers as the nationalists look to retain traditional structures and values in the face of the increasing Westernization in India driven by the growth in the middle class.

The protection of traditional structures is enshrined in legislation in India and many other nations. In India, the foreign direct investment laws require that a single-brand retailer must have 51% ownership in a joint venture and a multibrand retailer can only operate through a franchise model or a cash-and-carry, whole-business model.[16] This type of nationalism severely limits the opportunities for foreign business investment. The legislation will remain in place until the electorate in a democracy demands change or a ruling regime believes there are significant opportunities available by altering the legislation.

The implications for retailers include highlighting the provision of local produce where available, working within restrictive legislation in some areas, ensuring that staff and customer safety are a top priority, and identifying areas for growth that will allow for the control of business development.

Religious Fundamentalism

Recent events in global politics have identified religious fundamentalism as a force that can impact all elements of business and commerce. There are increased concerns with active protest, restrictive legislation, and, indeed, acts of terrorism in response to foreign business entry into a new culture or to the continued presence of international commerce in society (including retail businesses). There is a need for international retailers to understand the characteristics and driving values of religious fundamentalism around the globe. As of this date, there are few studies that have considered religion, fundamental or moderate, as a consideration for retailers.[17]

A study based on American data has looked at what happens to religious groups when confronted with competition from shopping malls.[18] The research examines the opportunity cost to the individual and to society lost from participation in a religious tradition of Sunday church attendance. In the United States, there are the so called blue laws that prohibit Sunday trading, and religious observance prohibits the individual from participating in commercial activities such as shopping. The legislation is in place in response to lobbying from activist Christian groups who wanted the retail environment to be responsive to their religious tenets, particularly in the observance of Sunday rituals.

In this case, the freedom of the individual is subjugated to the requirements of the church through the legislation, and the opportunity to shop on Sunday is withdrawn from the options available to the individual. This example is therefore a form of collective consumer resistance based on the framework of the religious community.

Nationalism is found in many countries and, combined with religious fundamentalism, can lead to active consumer rebellion.

Environmentalism

There are in existence many sophisticated groups—local, national, and international—who act as lobby groups for their particular environmental cause. Groups include the World Wildlife Fund, the Sea Shepherd Conservation Society, Friends of the Earth, and the Society for a Sustainable Future. These groups have a membership of many thousands who share common values. Members of these environmental groups may wish to boycott goods from poorer countries, not because they are concerned about job losses in the richer nations, but because they are concerned about the loss of the natural environment caused by deforestation and pollution. Further collective acts of consumer resistance in retail based on concern for the environment relate to the preservation of marine life, such as the successful campaigns to protect species such as dolphins from the tuna catch. Environmentalists can be highly politically engaged and will use technology to get their message through to their constituency. Environmental groups such as the World Wildlife Fund are highly influential, with a mature organizational structure operating in 100 countries. These groups are extending the reach of their debate for conservation by addressing issues of wildlife and climate change. Those individuals who hold very strong beliefs in the protection and conservation of wildlife and the environment are a force that needs to be considered by retailers. Their messages are heard globally and locally, and they have the resources to introduce protests and boycotts rapidly. Many retailers will be cognizant of these groups and will have taken steps as businesses and supply chain managers to deliver products that comply with consumer demands. The challenge for retailers will continue as environmentalists take collective action in relation to climate change generally and carbon production specifically. Retailers must be sensitive to environmental protection as part of their corporate social responsibility.

These forces of consumer resistance can be considered controversial as they go to the heart and soul of the belief structures of many groups in society. The reality is that nationalism, religious fundamentalism, and environmentalism, despite being underresearched, are forces in consumer resistance that are prevalent, powerful, and permanent. In the following section, we discuss motivations internal to the consumer and the role of these motivations in consumer resistance.

Internal Motivations

The second stage of our model relates to the micro-level internal motivations of the consumer, which are based on the values previously discussed.

Our research shows that internal motivations can lead to consumers seeking economic value, health, convenience, identity creation, and security and safety. Plus they search for identity resulting from their individual empowerment from participation in consumer collectives that can be local or global, virtual or physical.

Economic Value

Value for the retail customer is perceived in a number of ways. A customer may actively seek a product that provides value by being located in the deep-discount dollar stores. This same customer may seek value when seeking to purchase a luxury item. Customers have been actively seeking value in retail at both ends of the spectrum for several decades. This search for value has resulted in the polarization of the retail market from dollar stores to luxury, high-end boutiques. It should be noted that at both ends of the market, the customer is seeking value for money with reference to the quality of the product.

It is expected that customers will continue to seek value from retailers in response to difficult economic circumstances. An increased emphasis on value is evident in the rapid development of deep-discount retailing, which has been evident in the Western world for nearly a century. The consumer society (as discussed in Chapter 1) has led to many citizens believing that consumption will bring happiness and the more expensive the item, the more happiness will result. The search for value is an indication that a paradigm shift is taking place for some shoppers. For instance, in the past, shoppers were embarrassed to present coupons; however, this is no longer the case. In the United States, searches on Google for "printable coupons" increased by 186% in 2009 alone. Further, for the first time in 17 years, shoppers used more coupons than they did the year before, with 3.3 billion consumers' packaged goods coupons redeemed, a 27% increase over 2008.[19]

Health

Customer behavior, and sometimes resistance or minimization actions, can be driven by a desire for better health and well-being. Many customers desire improved health through careful scrutiny of their nutritional status. Other customers may be very concerned about stress in their lives and will consider downshifting to improve their health, which is also a form of personal empowerment. Customers will invest time and effort to gain knowledge of ways of consuming that minimize the negative impact on their bodies. The gaining of knowledge of impurities in foodstuffs can lead customers to different levels of resistance; for instance, they may avoid certain food types (i.e., seek out functional food types, such as organics). Functional food types can include added values, such as oils (i.e., omega 3), and properties aiding medical conditions, such as cholesterol-lowering margarines. Organic food options are also gaining wide spread traction in the market due to customer demand for a more holistic lifestyle via healthier eating, increased interest in food traceability, aversion to chemicals, and an overall return to basics. According to the Organic Trade Association's 2010 Organic Industry Survey, U.S. sales of organic food and beverages have grown from $1 billion in 1990 to $24.8 billion in 2009 (5.1% growth over 2008).[20] This trend has implications for all retailers for their corporate proposition, the selection of products on offer, and the messages portrayed to customers in marketing communications.

Convenience

In an increasingly time-poor society, customers are turning toward more convenient lifestyle and retailing options. This desire for convenience is not exclusively limited to stores, with customers expecting more convenient and time-efficient processes, locations, and store layouts from retailers in an attempt to balance the many competing tasks they face. This has also contributed to a related shift toward convenience foods and packaging. The retail industry has also witnessed significant growth in self-service technologies, ranging from store kiosks that enable customers to look up product information to self-checkout lanes, which enable customers to bypass long lines and process their own merchandise for purchase. Consumers are increasingly turning to a range of emerging channels such as websites, kiosks, and mobile phones to provide convenience in time and effort. Looking forward, an important consideration for retailers is their capability to develop new products and services that offer consumers the most convenience through the most appropriate channel.

Shopping trips are no longer an isolated event but rather are planned, and many consumers have begun performing more than one activity at a time. In a shopping context, this translates into multipurpose shopping or one-stop shopping and accounts for the success of retail facilities such as the supercenter. Trends such as these have been interpreted as indicating that to succeed in today's time-scarce environment, retail facilities must offer value for time in the same way they strive to offer value for money.[21] From the shopper's viewpoint, convenience therefore means an increase in the number of tasks that can be accomplished during a single shopping trip and a reduction in the time required to shop. The contemporary mall or shopping center therefore fulfils many criteria in terms of shopping convenience, which has been shown to be key in the minds of customers undertaking routine and regular shopping expeditions at mall locations[22] (meaning utilitarian shopping motivations as opposed to more recreational and hedonistic shopping motivations). These utilitarian trips might be to grocery stores, post offices, and banks.

Identity Creation

Many shoppers today are seeking the creation of their own unique identity through retail and brand experiences; often this is assisted in retail through personalization and cocreation experiences. Personalization and cocreation represent a fundamental shift in the way customers are resisting the mass market (or looking for ways to bypass goods that are perfectly made and off the shelf). In a traditional sense, personalization means the ability to define and therefore target products and services based on the interests of an individual. Today, however, it is more about the individual choosing from a range of options; it is a choice that says to the world at large, "This is me; this is who I am and what I stand for." Customers want products that are tailor-made to their own specific needs and wants, from coffee to running shoes. In this context, technology is making it much easier for retailers to get on the leading edge of customization. In discussions with senior retailers, we found that personalization was identified as a key theme moving into the future. In fact, many of our respondents discussed the fact that customers will increasingly resist the mainstream and seek to personalize their product, service, or experience. For instance,

> There is an opportunity for customer customization in store, which is happening around the world at different locations. And that leads into the automation side of things—robotics and the like—the fact that you can go and look at something online and then a robot will build it and ship it to you is becoming common place.[23]

Over the past 10 years, Build-A-Bear and American Girl Place have been successful examples of retail mass customization. More recently, Nike has introduced capabilities that allow customers to create their own shoes on its retail site within certain guidelines based on style and color. Catalogue retailer Lands' End allows customers to enter in their measurements in the "My Virtual Model" program. Although the company does not produce clothes customized for the individual shopper, customers can use the online virtual model to see how existing Lands' End clothing styles look on a particular body type. This virtual technology is able to be employed across a range of different retail stores and also beyond fashion—for instance, in modeling weight loss.

A successful online business primarily based on co-creation is Thread-less.com, which manufacturers a limited run of T-shirts that are designed by the customer and then submitted to the website for community vote. Every week, contestants upload their shirt designs to the site, where about 700 compete to be among the six that get printed. Site visitors then score designs on a 0 to 5 scale and the staff selects winners. In exchange for their creative input in T-shirt design, winning artists receive $2,000 in cash plus a $500 gift voucher (which they can trade in for $200 additional cash if preferred).

Another example of personalization was implemented by U.S. department store Macy's. The program seeks to better connect with the customer via regionally tailored programs that are more engaging and relevant.[24] In this instance, Macy's aims to convince customers that they are returning to an era of service when sales associates provide a personal and detailed service including personal invitations to store events. They are doing so by updating and expanding loyalty programs, which once rewarded shoppers only for frequent purchasing, and by offering locally relevant marketing and merchandising.

Security, Safety, and Risk Aversion

The topic of risk minimization has been researched by marketing academics for several decades, with recent research revealing that consumers feel more at risk when purchasing online via catalog or other media than they do when shopping in store.[25] In general terms, consumer perceptions of risk are heightened in multichannel formats. Some of the retail responses to managing perceptions of risk have included the development of online payment services, such as PayPal, and an increase in advertising about the product to relieve customer concerns.

Other consumer perceptions of risk can relate to health. For example, avoidance behavior can take place when individuals perceive a risk if they proceed with consumption. This is particularly evident with opposition to genetically modified (GM) foods. The campaign against GM foods has been particularly successful, with many individuals believing that these food types are potentially hazardous to their health.

Individuals will be cautious when considering the purchase of toxic substances, including certain laundry, kitchen, and general cleaning products. Gardening chemicals are sources of concern for potential purchasers. Customers will actively avoid products that require a high level of protection of personal safety or where the storage of products may result in a domestic security procedure. Hence a range of organic cleaning and gardening products are now a permanent feature of supermarket and hardware stores.

Security and risk are a personal and perennial topic for consumer research. As technologies and science provide new products that are not well understood, or the environment changes resulting in potential risks, the result will be consumer resistance.

Empowerment Through Collectives

The term "collective" can be used here to describe a group of connected customers. "Collective" in this context does not refer to people living across the street, but to online groups brought together using social network software to share interests, passions, beliefs, hobbies, or lifestyles. Often, these communities strive to gain empowerment in order to resist the market (e.g., to avoid purchase of full-priced items). The behaviors of these communities may range from price comparison and user review sites as part of pre-purchase research to more militant formations of dedicated buying groups in an effort to dictate market prices. The more extreme form of militant collectives attack corporations and brands they believe to be operating unscrupulously in a very public and organized manner; they are demanding, assertive, and extremely active. Such pressure groups and collective resistance groups are not new, but the recent ferocity of their assaults on retailers is unprecedented. Typically, the collective opinion is built on reviews, whereby customers exchange information and experiences on products and services, with most of this exchange now being done via the online channel. For instance, a senior retail executive commented that

> there are fashion websites that have people talking to each other and sharing information about sales and the like. Certainly when you buy products social networks or independent reviews can help

a lot. It's not just word of mouth from family and friends now, it's global and this has implications for brands. The good things and the good stories are amplified around the world, but likewise for bad stories. It's a dangerous way to go if you try to manipulate comments; those sorts of mistakes can be amplified quickly.[26]

The consumer now has the ability to participate freely and readily in these collectives. This can provide individuals with a sense of empowerment in their lives and in relation to their shopping. This empowerment is sought by many, and the existence and development of collectives is likely to become a permanent feature of the retail landscape.

Internal Experience

The third stage of our model relates to the micro-level internal experience of the consumer. Our model proposes that the internal experience of the consumer must align, or be in sync, with the consumer's internal motivations. If this alignment does not occur, there is a likelihood of conflict and a possibility of a resistant response. The internal experiences we pay particular attention to here, and are particularly relevant for retail, consist of the consumer experiencing boredom, cynicism, and even stress from too much choice. The possibility of conflict arises when there is a clash between consumer experience and value.

The shopper is seeking the following:

- An enjoyable experience
- Transparency in retail operations
- A minimal amount of stress and effort when shopping

Boredom

Customers today are overwhelmed by choice with an ever-increasing number of retail offers, each trying to be more creative and engaging than the last. Coupled with a rising number and variety of new retail concepts, many consumers have become desensitized, bored, and even resistant to traditional retailing. Many retailers have also decreased new product innovation efforts, resulting in a lack of novel products or designs. To combat this boredom and desensitization, customers are searching for a greater connection with retailers, and a more engaging retail experience, both online and in-store. This has further led to increasing demand for exclusive products that customers consider to be unique or of limited release, even if this means paying a price premium. When faced with a multitude of similar stores, customers will inevitably choose the one that is most in line with their wants, needs, brand preferences, and desire for engagement and entertainment. For retailers, this has placed increasing importance on understanding current consumer expectations and satisfaction, as well as experiential retailing elements.

Today's consumers are also seeking out variety in their purchases, trying new products, brands, and even new product categories. In 2007, TrendWatching[27], a consumer and business trend forecaster, identified a growing acceptance of consumers, increasingly saturated by the current retail environment, to venture out and try new products, dubbing the trend "trysumers" and predicting a growth in variety seeking in the coming years. Consumers are even seeking greater variety in the humble sandwich, with research suggesting up to 50% of consumers were dissatisfied with the sandwich options available to them at many stores.[28] Trysumers are more likely to respond to marketing that lowers the barriers of decision for a quick purchase and retail experiences that allow them to sample and experience products prior to purchasing.[29]

The boredom of customers also sheds light on the decline of the traditional shopping mall in the United States.[30] In the 1800s and early 1900s, downtown shopping was the typical location for retail as the infrastructure of the cities was established with transport into the available. Ease of access, safe and reliable parking, and a range of stores were essential to the success of shopping malls. The early shopping malls were designed with anchor tenants, generally a major department store at one end and a supermarket at the other. The role of the anchor tenants was to attract customers to visit the center and generate traffic through the mall. In the decades that followed, shopping malls were built all over the United States, with shoppers becoming desensitized to their proposition and the supply (or availability) of malls outpacing customer demand. This, in turn, resulted in difficulties for property developers and retailers to return a responsible profit and little investment in routine and preventable maintenance, which meant many malls began to look tired, unwelcoming, and lacking any kind of uniqueness.

Cynicism

Customers are increasingly cynical toward consumption and can, at times, actively resist the stimulus of the market. For instance, there are consumers who fear and distrust the market, including retailers, and are concerned that they will be deceived by advertisers and marketers. The cynicism can be the result of the failure of the buying experience, the constant bombardment from the advertising and marketing media, or input from others. Further, cynical customers may be challenging much of the consumer ideology that defines happiness based on the acquisition of material goods. Academics from the University of Lille in France, Philippe Odou and Pauline de Pechpeyrou, believe that cynicism can be seen as a defensive response to all-encompassing market forces, including the promises and promotions of brands and retailers. Their extended definition of customer cynicism asserts that the skeptical customer may not necessarily be an anticonsumer but may be seeking ethical or green behavior without success.[31]

Cynicism can also be the result of consumers' increasing brand literacy, with shoppers now able to deconstruct brand strategy and identify values that have been simply stated (i.e., "environmentally friendly" or "consumer champion") but not delivered. Savvy brands have avoided consumer cynicism by not taking themselves too seriously while tapping into genuine consumer insights. A recent spray-on deodorant advertising campaign by Australian deodorant brand Lynx is one such example. Taken literally, it communicates immediate success with the opposite sex, a claim that is unrealistic. However, the advertising adopts a tongue-in-cheek delivery of the message, which has given the brand widespread acceptance among male audiences. Apple is another successful brand in that it was originally perceived as a brand for nerds, by nerds, but with the birth of the first iMac, the brand set out to change that. By considering home computing from a different perspective, Apple embarked on a long-term plan to reposition what having a computer in your home was all about. Over 10 years later, the iPod has done the same for listening to music. A quick scan down the main street in any city center will reveal the vast number of people sporting white earphones, not the generic, black variety.[32]

Too Much Choice

Stress is endemic in contemporary society, with long working hours, disrupted families, and highlighted economic and political pressures. Customers are seeking a retail environment that is relaxed and relatively stress free, in clean and accessible surroundings. Confusion resulting from too much choice can lead to undue stress in customers as they shop. The challenge arises when the array of brands, assortments, and sizes of items becomes overwhelming to customers and they make no choice in the fear of making the wrong choice in the face of so many. This sense of being overwhelmed by choice is an output of the industrial consumer society and, as such, has been studied for several decades.

Alvin Toffler,[33] American writer and futurist, first coined the term "overchoice" and discussed that such stresses can lead to poor decision making, confusion, or consumer resistance in the form of not purchasing at all. The types of environment where overchoice may occur are often found in the modern supermarket. Take, for example, the array of choices in sizes, brands, flavors, additives, and calorific values of tubs of yogurt or the aisles of chips of every different flavor combination, size, shape, and presentation. Customers looking for a simple yogurt or bag of chips might shake their heads in dismay at the number of choices available. The concept of overchoice was revisited by Barry Schwartz in 2004 in his book *The Paradox of Choice*,[34] in which he argues that happiness is not found in 30 different types of camera and indeed that the range of choices can lead to customers being dissatisfied and regretting the choices they made. Social psychologists Sheena Iyengar and Mark Lepper [35] ran a number of empirical studies that found that people were more highly motivated when able to select from a group of approximately six items as opposed to 24–30 items. Their studies revealed that participants not only were more highly motivated but also actually performed better when presented with a limited choice of options.

Conflict

The fourth part of our model relates to the conflict consumers experience when their internal motivations are not met by their experience, be it a personal experience with a retailer or an evaluation of a retailer's activities. Conflict may occur in a number of situations where the customer's values are not met or are out of alignment. For example, a customer may resist purchasing organic products when the price is significantly higher than alternative products that may not advertise their organic status or may contain additives that are not regarded as acceptable by the customer.

This conflict leads to the final stage of our model, response, which may be mainstream or fringe, and is detailed in the next chapter.

To summarize, when there is a conflict between individuals' values and their encountered retail experience, there is a possibility of a response in a form of resistance.

CHAPTER 5

Responses

Mainstream and Fringe

The global retail and consumer environment is characterized by high levels of turbulence and fragmentation. Within this challenging backdrop, there is a need for retailers (as well as all consumer-facing organizations) to establish ways to make sense of what is occurring, and it is important to develop an understanding of what is occurring not only in the mainstream but also on the fringe.

Consumer resistance movements have arguably moved from the fringe to become more mainstream, partly facilitated by the digital age. Globally, consumers are collectively gathering and taking on corporations in a variety of ways, and these activities can be broadly categorized as mainstream or fringe. Mainstream activities include lifestyle movements centered on finding a more simple, and sustainable, lifestyle in response to the capitalist economy (i.e., downshifting, voluntary simplifying, and slow living), consumer boycotts and consumer cooperatives. Mainstream activities include lifestyle movements centered on finding a more simple, and sustainable, lifestyle in response to the capitalist economy (i.e., downshifting, voluntary simplifying, and slow living), Consumer boycotts and consumer cooperatives. Fringe activities tend to be political and social movements against corporate dominance and include culture jamming, antiglobalization, antisweatshop, anti–chain store, and antitechnology movements. All these movements show the importance of consumer resistance in the construction of modern consumer identities.[1]

It is important to recount here that, generally speaking, the choices and practices of resistant consumers (in terms of retailing) are centered on the search ethical, green, or activist lifestyles. It is also important to highlight that consumer resistance is both an activity and an attitude. It is an activity of refusal that can range from the polite "I would prefer not to buy" to the explicit 1968 French slogan "Soyons realists, demandons l'impossible" ("Be realistic, demand the impossible"). It is also an attitude that declines to give recognition to the ideology of progress and material growth.[2]

Mainstream Movements

As noted previously, consumerism is conventionally understood as refer-ring not to the consumption of goods and services per se, but to the endless desire and routinely wasteful consumption of affluent econo-mies.[3] As a result, a range of sociopolitical consumer movements has emerged against equating personal happiness with consumption and the purchase of material possessions. Through collective action, consum-ers can directly influence the mode of consumption from attempting to determine the price, quality, and availability of goods and services to boy-cotting and forming cooperatives to control the provision of goods and services. We draw on an existing continuum of consumer resistance to classify mainstream resistance. This continuum[4] suggests that there are three main categories of resistance: avoidance (i.e., not buying), mini-mization (i.e., downshifting), and active rebellion (i.e., boycotting). Our discussion of mainstream consumer resistance draws on this continuum to represent the dynamic nature of the phenomena and conveys how the attitudes and actions of the customer can change. We present the con-tinuum of resistance in Figure 5.1, and in the remainder of this section we discuss and extend the individual components of the model.

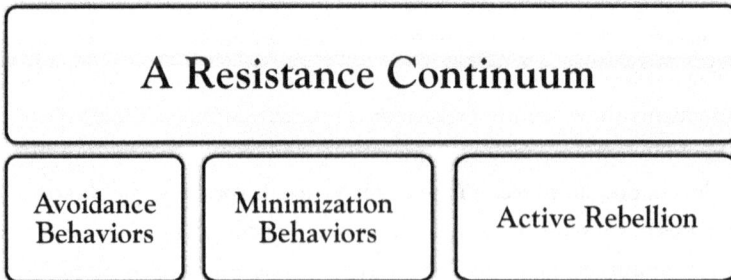

A Resistance Continuum

| Avoidance Behaviors | Minimization Behaviors | Active Rebellion |

Figure 5.1. A Continuum of Consumer Resistance
Source: Adapted from Fournier (1998), pp. 88–91.

Avoidance Behaviors

Consumers may be resistant in the form of avoidance because of a dislike of certain brands. This avoidance behavior may be based on unsatisfactory experiences or when the brand is incongruent with the consumer's self-identity. It could also be a moral avoidance, such as when there is a perceived clash between the values of the individual or society and the actions and values associated with the brand.[5] Some brands are avoided due to personal reasons, while others are avoided because of their perceived impact on a global scale. After 5 years of research, marketing academic Mike Lee at Auckland University has identified the scientific rationale behind such behavior and suggests the interplay of four factors: how a brand fits with our lifestyle, its value for money, our past experiences, and our moral beliefs. Interestingly, his research showed clothing brands and car makers were most affected by identity avoidance and value-for-money issues, as consumers avoided a product if it did not reflect their personality or lifestyle. One respondent said he avoided wearing Nike shoes because of the bad press it received regarding its sweat shops: "It's almost like you can be frowned upon wearing Nike these days, because (some think) there's irresponsibility that goes with buying and supporting a brand like that."[6]

Another form of brand avoidance relates to the vast array of counterfeit luxury brands produced and marketed. The copying of luxury goods has led to problems with individuals not having confidence that the item they are purchasing is authentic. This has resulted in shoppers avoiding Prada, Gucci, Louis Vuitton, and other high-end brands not because they cannot afford them but because they do not think the brand is worth the price given the popularity of counterfeits.[7] At the same time, many individuals are more than happy to purchase the knock off Gucci and Yves Saint Laurent handbags with the full knowledge of its status and present it to the world in this way. There can be a lack of clarity about authenticity, and the presence of many scounterfeits can therefore lead to devaluation of the luxury brand. Some individuals will choose not to consume, as the authenticity and value of the brand is difficult to ascertain.

Avoiding the New

Another form of avoidance is driving demand in the secondhand space, with pursuits such as secondhand shopping and consumers' desire to avoid mainstream fashion, which is driving both offline and online secondhand shopping (i.e., facilitated by platforms such as eBay). For many, these activities underlie an individual's search for uniqueness or retro chic. Furthermore, finding things by yourself can result in a level of attachment to the object, particularly during the early days of possession, sometimes purely because the item has subjective novelty value to the individual[8] and has never previously being owned. Secondhand shopping can encourage a hunter-gather mentality, with the act inspiring the consumer to search for a bargain or some unique or one-off item. Secondhand clothing or the recycling of clothes is nothing new; however, sales of vintage and secondhand clothing have gained significant popularity with a very wide sociodemographic shopping at Goodwill stores. One key driver for this activity is the rise of reworking and refashioning of such items. While many consumers love secondhand and vintage clothing just as they are, refashioning them into new pieces has the benefit of creating completely unique, designer, and cutting edge. At its roots, the trend has its origins in secondhand fashion stores, where clothing is (often in the case of charity) donated by one person and resold to another. However, the trend is becoming mainstream, with some fashion labels using recycled clothes to create new items. One example is London-based Junky Styling, an early adopter of the trend toward deconstructing traditional clothing from charity shops and jumble sales to form tailored pieces. Since 1997, Sanders and Seager of Junky Styling have been melding edgy design and the do-it-yourself (DIY) spirit after discovering the prevalence of recycling from San Francisco to Tokyo following their world travels in their early twenties. The pair first started making experimental outfits to go clubbing and dressing their friends, and after opening a stall in Kensington Market, the business grew and moved into its present hub in East London's Brick Lane. All items are recreated and handcrafted from deconstructed, preowned garments and no two items are the same.

Avoiding Help: Doing It Yourself

Many consumers today are seeking alternatives to traditional consumerism, striving to get back to basics and create products for themselves, by themselves, ranging from fashion items to home renovations. What is important about this behavior is not necessarily the final product but the process involved. Sociologist Colin Campbell calls it *craft consumption.*[9] Craft consumption refers to the production of something made and designed by the same person. It has its roots in the traditional notions of craft first conceptualized by thinkers such as Karl Marx through the alienation of the production processes of industrialization. Via craft consumption, consumers create an overall ensemble, whereby a number of different goods can be combined and built to be something new (a new entity)—for instance, a complete room or an entire outfit of clothing. Through this, consumers are increasingly creating their own individual and unique world of meaning and, at the same time, strengthening their personal connection to the object made. The connection between consumers and objects facilitated by the process of DIY is evident in IKEA's flat-pack (component part) proposition. Essentially, consumers play an active role in the production and consumption experience, even though IKEA products are globally standardized. Consumers are left to interpret final products and to acquire a sense of belonging toward those goods through specific rituals, such as carrying them home and assembling them. So while the consumption of IKEA furniture is, as described by the protagonist in the 1999 film *Fight Club*,[10] "a bid to reproduce the lifestyles laid down in the magazine-style phone catalogues," in the end, the ownership of a standardized piece of furniture becomes personal, with greater meaning assigned via the creation process.

The perceived saving for the consumer is the (essentially zero) cost of labor involved in design and product of goods; however, there is a paradox in terms of the final cost of manufacture, where the total cost of the components can far exceed the cost of the final product. This paradox does not however, diminish the value of DIY in terms of individual identity and personal satisfaction as a result of the process.

In today's marketplace, there are a number of different factors that might drive DIY consumption behavior. These include a consumer's desire for uniqueness (through the creation of individual artifacts), the creation of self-identity (through DIY home renovations), and a desire to minimize the impact of consumption on the environment (through minimizing waste to landfill). The latter of these factors is particularly relevant in the fashion sector, where there is a groundswell of consumers taking personal control of minimizing the effects of fast fashion on the environment. Fast fashion (the clothing equivalent of fast food) provides the marketplace with affordable apparel; however, it is perceived by many as detrimental to the environment. Fuelling the fashion demand, magazines, celebrities, and the media help create the desire for new must-have items each season. However, a significant downside of the trend is the pollution footprint left behind in the clothing life cycle through environmental and occupational hazards. For example, polyester, made from petroleum, is widely used in the clothing manufacturing process. The manufacture of polyester is an energy-intensive process requiring large amounts of crude oil. In the United States, much of the cotton produced is exported to China, among other countries, where the material is milled, woven into fabrics, cut, and assembled according to preset specifications. In her 2005 book *The Travels of a T-Shirt in the Global Economy*, Georgetown University professor Pietra Rivoli[11] writes that each year, Americans purchase approximately one billion clothing garments made in China, the equivalent of four pieces of clothing for every U.S. citizen.

In the book *Waste and Want: A Social History of Trash*, University of Delaware historian of American consumer culture Susan Strasser traces the progressive obsolescence of clothing and other consumer goods to the 1920s. The book argues that before the 1920s, most clothing was repaired, mended, tailored to fit other family members, or recycled within the home as rags or quilts. However, the spirit of conservation did not last long into the 20th century, and today the path that an item of clothing travels from the sales floor to the landfill is much shorter. However, the journey of a piece of clothing does not always end in a landfill. A portion of clothing purchases are recycled mainly in three ways: clothing may be (a) exported in bulk for sale in developing countries, (b) chemically or mechanically recycled into raw material for the manufacture of other apparel and nonapparel products, or (c) resold by the primary consumer to other consumers at a lower price.

From a practical standpoint, and set against the backdrop of DIY consumerism, recent trends reveal the increasing role fashion has played in the DIY home-renovation sector. In particular, new product ranges have combined fashion with megabrands including Martha Stewart, Ralph Lauren, and boutique New Zealand fashion designer Karen Walker. Building on this, recent years have seen consumers seeking to take control of many aspects of consumption from DIY in the context of home to DIY in fashion or food.

Minimization Behaviors

Minimization behaviors, according to Fournier,[12] can consist of two strategies: coping and downsizing. In terms of coping strategies, resistance behaviors can take place when individuals perceive a risk from their consumption (as discussed earlier in terms of GM foods).

Downsizers—sometimes known as voluntary simplifiers—are, according to Australian academics Margaret Craig-Lees and Constance Hill,[19] individuals, acting either alone or as part of a social movement, who for whatever reason choose to live with fewer material goods. The voluntary simplifier can be part of a collective such as the consumer activity groups evident since the 1970s. Other voluntary simplifiers include baby boomers (born between 1945 and 1965). These groups are beginning to retire and are changing the size and number of their material goods as they downsize by selling the family home for an apartment or retirement condominium. This results in the disposal of furniture and domestic goods, as the new accommodation is generally much smaller. This group is sometimes regarded as resistant, indeed as anticonsumption, as they have all the material goods that they require and would prefer to spend their income on travel and services. Other voluntary simplifiers experience a range of motivations and may not belong to any particular social movement. The underlying motivation may be a tendency toward frugality and simplicity.

Some individuals develop a sense of heroism as they pursue the change in their lifestyles. The voluntary simplifier is resisting the tongue in cheek, new millennium expression Descartes of "I shop, therefore I am."[20] An understanding of voluntary simplifiers can lead to new or revised marketing strategies to provide goods and services that are appropriate and acceptable to them. Such strategies may increase the total market size and provide avenues for new or modified products and services.

The Waste-Not Mentality

There are many different motivations behind consumers' desire to minimize waste through their consumption activities, or what we call a *waste-not* mentality. Traditionally these motivations have been economic, environmental, and social.

Economic motivations relate often to reduction or elimination of spending and the resultant saving of money. This is often achieved by individuals constructing the desired object through purchasing and assembling component parts themselves rather than purchasing the completed product. This motivation to reduce expenditure was exacerbated by the 2009 global financial crisis and a subsequent desire to save. Environmental motivations vary, but include reducing waste through either the reduction of unnecessary packaging or the reduction in waste to landfill. Social motivations are typically centered on the greater good for the community, the people within it, and future generations.

Economic, environmental, and social motivations, by their very nature, assume rational consideration by the consumer. For instance, an economic explanation of DIY behavior could easily be a consumer's inability to afford to pay for external labor; however, this rational perspective undermines the emotional and aspirational elements of such a decision. Australian academic Ian Woodward[16] says DIY can be a means for individuals to realize effects that convey individuality and self-identity. These motivations are therefore part of the search for greater meaning in one's life beyond consumption for the sake of it.

Over the past decade, we have seen a boom in DIY activities. These activities are the outward manifestation of the move known as cocooning. Primarily driven by the preglobal financial crisis buoyant housing market, it has been represented by the rise in television home makeover and property development media. In the housing market, a waste-not culture extends to DIY home improvement activities undertaken by the home owner rather than by employing professional help and may include building, renovating, painting, decorating, and landscaping.

When combined with trends toward nostalgia and cocooning, the DIY market will continue to grow.

Downshifting

The downshifting movement has emerged largely as a response to the frenetic pace of modern life and has been exacerbated by changes in the global economy. By definition, downshifting is a social behavior in which individuals seek to live simpler lives to escape the obsessive and excessive pursuit of money and materialism. Studies have uncovered a number of primary motivations, including a desire for a more balanced and sustainable life, poor health as a result of excessive stress at work, escaping the work-and-spend cycle, and removing the clutter of unnecessary possessions.[17] Further, the search for improved health and the desire to spend money and time meaningfully (as opposed to wastefully or without thought) are core values of downshifting. In practice, downshifting involves a variety of behavioral and lifestyle changes, including downshifts in work and income, spending habits, or environmental impact and or by geographically relocating, for instance from the city to the coast. The downshifter is generally still enmeshed in the consumer society and will seek a whole new range of goods and services to support their new lifestyle. The downshifter will consume differently, and the consumer markets, such as the small office–home office (SOHO) market, have emerged as a result of downshifting.

Because downshifting is fundamentally based on dissatisfaction with the consequences of the work environment,[18] the most common form of downshifting is related to changes in employment (or income). The philosophy of working to live replaces the dominant social ideology of living to work. The associated reorienting of economic priorities tips the scale of the work-life balance away from the workplace. Economically, work downshifts are defined in terms of reductions in income, work hours, and spending levels[19] in favor of gaining other nonmaterial benefits. On an individual level, work downshifting is a voluntary reduction in annual income and therefore time spent at work as part of the quest for a more meaningful life outside of work.[20] Career downshifts are another way of downshifting economically and entail lowering previous aspirations of wealth, promotion, or higher social status[21] and may include quitting a job to work in the local community, to work from home, or to start a small business.

Being a careful, thoughtful consumer or actively practicing alternative forms of consumption is another aspect of downshifting. For example, a customer may choose to purchase only necessities as a way to focus on quality of life. This consumer will try not to purchase goods for emotional or aspirational motivations and will seek personal identity and satisfaction in other ways.[22] This realignment of spending priorities promotes the functional utility of goods over their ability to convey status, which is evident in downshifters being, in general, less brand-conscious.[23] These consumption habits also facilitate the option of working and earning less because annual spending is proportionally lower. Consumption downshifting may include alternative dietary choices and supplements, which include buying local foods, raising food-producing animals like chickens, and planting a sustainable garden, lowering the cost of food by minimizing food miles and significantly reducing the transaction costs of trips to the supermarket.[24]

The downshifting movement is most popular in the United States, the United Kingdom, and Australia, with approximately 20%–25%[25] of each country's consumers identifying themselves in this way. Clive Hamilton[26], author and professor of public ethics refers to downshifters as people who voluntarily make lifestyle changes which result in accepting significantly less income and consuming less. His study in 2003 revealed that, contrary to widely held beliefs, downshifters are as likely to be blue-collar workers as white-collar workers. This is supported by international research that demonstrates that downshifting attracts participants across the socioeconomic spectrum.[27] According to Tracey Smith, British founder of International Downshifting Week, writer and broadcaster, the scope of participation is limitless because all members of society—adults, children, businesses, institutions, organizations, and governments—are able to downshift.[28]

A recent survey conducted in the United States showed that 19% of adult Americans had voluntarily reduced their income and consumption levels in the past 5 years.[29] Similarly, the Australian Institute reported in 2003 that 23% of adult Australians had downshifted to a simpler lifestyle on less income over the past 10 years. Similar findings have been reported in New Zealand and Canada. A survey in the United Kingdom in 2004 revealed that 4 out of 10 people under the age of 35 are planning to leave their high-powered, high-stress jobs and downshift at some point during their careers. A November 2004 poll conducted by *US News and World Report* found that 48% of Americans have done at least one of the following in the past 5 years: (a) cut back their hours at work, (b) declined or did not seek a promotion, (c) lowered their expectations for what they need out of life, (d) reduced their work commitments, or (e) moved to a community with a less hectic way of life.[30]

Downshifting is a significant consumer movement; however, there can be a disconnect between what people are planning to do and what they actually do. It would appear that further empirical research is needed to better understand the drivers behind downshifting and the implications for society at large.

Voluntary Simplifying

In the 1990s, voluntary simplifying, or the simple-living movement, began appearing in mainstream media and has continually grown in popularity among populations living in industrial societies, especially the United States, the United Kingdom, and Australia (as this behavior is closely linked to downshifting). As the term suggests, simple living is a voluntary lifestyle choice characterized by consuming only that which is required to sustain life. Similar to downshifting, simple living is a response to consumerism, materialism, and the modern quest for affluence. Participants may choose to live their lives in this way for a variety of personal reasons, such as spirituality, health, increase in quality time with family and friends, reduction of their personal ecological footprint, stress reduction, personal taste, or frugality. Interestingly, simple living has traditions that stretch back to the Asia and the Middle East, espoused by leaders such as Zarathustra, Buddha, Laozi, and Confucius and was also evident in both Greco-Roman culture and Judeo-Christian ethics.[31]

The grassroots awareness campaign National Downshifting Week, begun in 1995, encourages participants to *positively embrace living with less*. Campaign creator, Tracey Smith says, "The more money you spend, the more time you have to be out there earning it and the less time you have to spend with the ones you love." National Downshifting Week encourages participants to "Slow Down and Green Up" and contains a list of suggestions for individuals, companies, children, and schools to help adopt green or eco-friendly policies and habits, develop corporate social and environmental responsibility in the workplace, and create eco-protocols and lessons that work alongside the national curriculum, respectively. Another practice is the adoption of a simplified diet, which may involve simplified domestic food production and consumption or veganism and the Gandhi diet. Yet another way to simplify life is to get back to the land and grow your own food. Self-sufficiency, in this way, can reduce dependency on money and the economy.

Retailers can respond to the voluntary simplifier by taking care of the disposal of excess goods. The growth of secondhand Goodwill-style stores is dependent on a supply of reasonable secondhand goods that can often be sourced from the downshifter or the voluntary simplifier. Customers respond to perceived pressures inherent in the consumer society and are looking to simplify their lives.

Slow Living

The slow-living movement is as a reaction against the frenzied pace of modern life and advocates a cultural shift toward slowing down life's pace. It is also an expression of nostalgia and cocooning and is a macro-level trend that can result in consumer resistance. The development of the slow-living movement has been enhanced and developed through the increase in consumer physical, social, and cultural mobility. Although it has existed in some form since the Industrial Revolution, the slow move-ment has grown considerably since the rise of slow food and Cittaslow (literally Slow City) in Europe, with slow initiatives spreading as far as Australia and Japan. Over time, this movement has developed into a sub-culture in other areas, such as slow schools, slow travel, slow shopping, slow art, slow gardening, and slow parenting.

Several large slow-living efforts have emerged with considerable fol-lowings, such as Slow Down Now and The World Institute of Slowness. The Sloth Club, founded in 1999 in Japan, is regarded as the leader of the slow movement in that country with many related initiatives, including Candlenight (where over 10 million participants turn off their lights and use candles for 2 hours), the slow business school (teaching the mantra of respecting the environment and human lives), and a network of cafe slows (slow food cafes). Many other smaller groups are cropping up around the globe. The International Institute of Not Doing Much (IINDM) is an approach to time poverty, incivility, and workaholism through humor and storytelling. First created in 2005, SlowDownNow.org is a continually evolving work of art and humor that reports it has 3,000 members. Author Christopher Richards is at work on *The International Institute of Not Doing Much's Guide to Slowing Down.*

There are a number of slow submovements relevant to this text. Opposed to the culture of fast food, slow food seeks to encourage the enjoyment of regional produce, traditional foods, which are often grown organically, and enjoying foods in the company of others. It aims to defend agricultural biodiversity. The movement claims 83,000 members in 50 countries, which are organized into 800 *convivia*, or local chapters. Sometimes operating under a logo of a snail, the collective philosophy is to preserve and support traditional ways of life. Today, 42 states in the United States have their own *convivium.*

Interest in the number of miles that food has been transported is part of slow food movements that are seeking locally grown food. This is now gaining mainstream acceptance, as shown by the popularity of books such as *The 100-Mile Diet* and Barbara Kingsolver's *Animal, Vegetable, Miracle: A Year of Food Life.* In each of these cases, the authors devoted a year to reducing their carbon footprint by eating locally.[32]

Slow travel is an evolving movement that has taken its inspiration from 19th-century European travel writers, such as Théophile Gautier, who reacted against the cult of speed, prompting some modern analysts to ask, "If we have slow food and slow cities, then why not slow travel?"[33] Advocates of slow travel argue that all too often the potential pleasure of the journey is lost by too eager anticipation of arrival. Slow travel, it is asserted, is a state of mind that allows travelers to engage more fully with communities along their route, often favoring visits to spots enjoyed by local residents rather than merely following guidebooks. As such, slow travel shares some common values with ecotourism. Its advocates and devotees generally look for low-impact travel styles, even to the extent of eschewing flying.

Slow art is an evolving movement championed by such proponents as Michael Kimmelman, chief art critic and columnist for the *New York Times.* It advocates appreciating an art work in itself as opposed to a rapid, flitting witnessing of art common in a hectic societal setting. One of its central tenets is that people often seek out what they already know as opposed to allowing the artist to present a journey or piece in its entirety.

Slow media is a movement aimed at sustainable and focused media production and consumption. It formed in the context of a massive acceleration of news distribution ending in almost real-time digital media such as Twitter. Beginning in 2010, many local slow media initiatives formed in the United States and Europe (Germany, France, Italy), leading to high attention to mass media. Others experiment with a reduction of their daily media intake and log their efforts online (known as a Slow Media Diet).

Active Rebellion

In terms of active rebellion, Fournier[34] notes that there are three types: complaining, boycotting, and dropping out. Protesting about some event or characteristic of a retail offer is an accepted activity in modern society. It is well known that customers will use word-of-mouth on many occasions if they are dissatisfied with a brand or store. Consumer grudge holding and retaliation is based on a perception that the store or brand has offended or harmed the consumer in some way, resulting in strongly felt emotions held by the consumer. IKEA, the furniture and housewares chain, has been subject to criticism because of its race track store layout that compels customers to travel throughout the store regardless of their in-store destination. This layout is compounded by walled displays that have been known to leave the customer disoriented. As one customer reports,

> When we came out, we weren't at the entrance, so we had to go back out to the right, through the checkout and there was no proper exit, you had to walk through the check out again even though we didn't have anything, back into the main entrance area and back to the internal center elevator to get back to the car park. It was awful; I don't think I will ever go back there again.[35]

This customer is clearly irritated by the experience and holds a grudge not to return to the store. This disgruntled customer is eclipsed by the retaliatory mood of another young customer: "They just didn't give two hoots and I'd been buying their clothes for ten years and I never will again. And I will tell all my friends, don't buy their jeans. I'm a very vindictive consumer in that way."[36]

These two customers demonstrate the power of individuals who are personally annoyed or offended by their store experience and will not purchase at these stores again. The power of word-of-mouth is important in complaining behavior, with customers now able to communicate their dissatisfaction quickly and globally via social networks and mobile technologies and therefore is no longer restricted to small groups of friends.

Retailers need to be aware that social media such as Facebook are being used to spread the word about retail experiences (both positive and negative). Therefore, the spread of word of mouth is now global and instant.

Boycotts

Consumer boycotts are used by various political- and social-awareness groups and individual consumers in an effort to effect change or simply to punish a company, nation, or brand for a perceived injustice.[37] Examples include consumer boycotts of French products because of nuclear testing in the Pacific, anti-Nike protests resulting from to news of sweat shop child labor being used to manufacture Nike products in South East Asia, the boycott of Harrods (the UK retailer) for stocking fur products, and a boycott against food manufacturers and agricultural suppliers for the marketing of GM foods. Consumer boycotts are studied as a collective activity crossing geographic and national borders. Consumer boycotts are feared by corporations and nations as they have proven in some cases to be successful in reducing markets and profitability or halting production, as well as damaging the brand. In the case of the biggest retailer in world, the U.S. discount giant Walmart, boycotters have formed their own online communities (affectionately named Hell-Mart) and produced anti-corporate movies, such as *Walmart: The High Cost of Low Price*.[38] Other retailers have experienced similar boycott action, including Starbucks ("I hate Starbucks") and McDonalds ("McSpotlight"). Consumer motivations for participating or not participating (and to what extent) in boycotting include the desire to make a difference, the scope for self-enhancement, counterarguments that inhibit boycotting, and the cost to the boycotter of constrained consumption.[39] The length and severity of a boycott can affect the health of the boycotted party or industries and therefore the jobs of the people employed by them. Boycotts of consumer products are generally triggered by a corporate policy or action and are designed to effect change, accomplish punishment, or both. Boycotts can therefore severely affect a company's profit margin and result in the loss of jobs.[40]

Boycotts have become more potent in recent decades with the development technology via Internet websites, blogs, Usenet newsgroups, and e-mail mailing lists. Indeed, within a matter of hours, consumer watchdog groups can arrange for thousands of consumers to boycott a product with a simple e-mail message. Target in the United States has experienced just this as part of a shareholder review of a US$150,000 donation made to Minnesota Forward, a group indirectly supporting antigay views. Despite an apology letter from chairman, president, and CEO Gregg Steinhafel on the Target website, the backlash was accelerated by social media and online communities. The "Boycott Target Until They Cease Funding Anti-Gay Politics" page on Facebook, created by progressive political group MoveOn.org, has more than 72,400 supporters and is growing. There were also protests at Target stores and at Target-sponsored events. MoveOn.org kept up the momentum through a 30-second ad protesting corporate donations in general and Target in particular. An animated ad, available on YouTube, features a stick figure with the Target bull's-eye for a head, pushing a shopping cart in which it collects members of Congress, the Republican elephant, and the Democratic donkey, the Statue of Liberty and an American flag, with a voice-over ending with "Boycott Target: Our democracy is not for sale."[41]

In modern times, with the advent of technologies such as social media, any business can be the target of consumer boycotts. An understanding of boycotts can therefore assist brands and retailers to devise strategies to limit the extent and possible damages they can cause.

Dropping Out

Dropping out, Fournier's[42] third type of active rebellion, can refer to those people who decide not to participate in the consumer society at all. For example, the ascetic will, for religious or moral reasons, seek personal fulfillment by eschewing the material world. Dropping out is a strong form of identity creation, and an internal motivation from the consumer resistance model. People who drop out are taking active steps to not be part of the consumer society and are establishing their own identities outside of the market forces. A well known example is political and ideological leader of India during the Indian independence movement, Mahatma Gandhi, with many others who continue to seek enlightenment through extreme simplicity in life. An American group of people who remain focused on production rather than consumption are the Amish, a group of Christian church fellowships that form a subgroup of the Mennonite churches. This group of individuals deliberately chose to avoid unnecessary consumption, although they participate in the market economy via their artisan skills. The Amish are avid recyclers and have a minimum footprint on the environment. In the true sense, the Amish have not dropped out, as they have never connected to the consumer society. The Amish lifestyle is not preferred by many citizens, and other routes to minimize consumption are sought. For example, some people go "off the grid," in that they choose neither to be connected to utilities such as electricity and gas, nor to purchase goods commercially, preferring instead to trade and exchange locally. These people are seeking self-sufficiency for a variety of personal and religious reasons, generally in more remote rural locations. Examples from contemporary societies include those individuals or groups who chose not to consume for a period such as The Christmas Resistance and the many Buy Nothing Day groups who collectively will cut up credit cards, the French Mouvement Anti-Noel, and the English movement Enough.

It is evident then that there are many motivations and ways to participate in activities that reduce consumption. Further, there are individuals and groups who move through the spectrum of resistance. Sometimes individual consumers will participate only for a period of time, through to those individuals who make life long commitments to consuming less or consuming differently.

Consumers therefore act either individually or collectively to express their concerns with regard to particular aspects of consumer society.

Consumer Cooperatives

Consumer resistance to corporate power can directly influence the supply of products to the market. For instance, cooperatives are socially owned and operated organizations that operate, theoretically at least, on a nonprofit basis in the provision of goods and services to the market. Cooperatives are businesses which are owned by its customers for mutual benefit, typically centered on price and quality. Resistance, and cooperative supply, spans many industries, including health care, insurance, credit unions, agricultural, and utility cooperatives. In the United States, Seattle-based PCC Natural Markets, a consumer-owned food cooperative, and Recreation Equipment Inc., which specializes in outdoor sporting equipment, are large and successful consumer cooperatives. In practice, cooperatives price goods and services at competitive market rates and retain accumulated capital in common ownership, distribute it to meet the consumer's social objectives, or refund this sum to the consumer/owner as an overpayment.

Consumer collaboration via the establishment of cooperative groups is a form of market control becoming increasingly common. Take for instance Boulder, Colorado–based *eSwarm*, a company that aims to bring buyers and sellers together with a model similar to bulk-buying clubs. Essentially, buyers register for a free account then join current swarms (groups of buyers), or create new ones, to focus on any consumer good, debt refinancing, prepaid gift and debit cards, and even insurance products. Sellers then bid for the business. This is essentially a way in which consumers are taking control and making the market bid for their business, which flips the traditional retail model on its head.

Fringe Movements

Kim Humphrey, from RMIT University in Australia, has explored the positive advances of the anticonsumerism movement amid the global recession in his book *Excess: Anti-consumerism in the West*. The book discusses the backlash and the varied approaches anticonsumerist activists take to inspire and promote different attitudes toward consumption through interviews with activists on three continents. Various trends in response to Western hyperconsumption are identified, including culture jamming, downshifting, and the more recent slow-living shift, as a response to the fast pace of modern life, demonstrating the proliferation of these movements globally. Fringe activities tend to be political and social movements against corporate dominance and include culture jamming (or antiadvertising) and the antiglobalization, antisweatshop, anti–chain store, and antitechnology movements. All these movements show the importance of anticonsumption practices in the construction of modern consumer identities.[43]

Antiadvertising

Culture jamming is a consumer social movement that aims to expose assumptions behind commercial culture and the branded environment, often by subverting and refiguring logo and product images.[44] This social movement can be traced as far back as the 1950s,[45] when *New York Times* columnist Mark Dery's article "The Merry Pranksters and the Art of the Hoax" first mentioned culture jamming in the mainstream media. Many retail brands are the subject of culture jamming; for example, Whirl-Mart, which is a culture jamming ritual aimed at retail superstores and described by participants as "art and action."[46] The Whirl-Mart culture jamming event consists of a group of supposed shoppers who congregate at a large superstore (usually a Wal-Mart, Toys 'R Us, Asda, or Sainsbury's), slowly push empty shopping carts through store aisles, not purchase anything, and form a lengthy chain of nonshoppers—weaving and "whirling" through a maze of store aisles for hours at a time. While most culture jamming focuses on subverting or critiquing political or advertising messages, some practitioners focus on a more positive, creative form of jamming that brings together artists, scholars, and activists to create new forms of cultural production that transcend rather than merely criticize the status quo.[47] Nonetheless, culture jamming is a form of disruption that plays on the emotions of viewers to evoke behavioral change and political action.

Over the years, advertising has become the focus for many culture jammers around the world, given advertising's control over many cultural spaces. This has been largely a reaction to both technological developments and consumer responses to advertising saturation. In turn, consumers have developed ad-avoidance strategies by filtering out excess advertising clutter. The Canadian magazine *Adbusters* provides a forum for critical views on consumerism and advertising through a focus on environmental, social, and psychological issues,[48] In lieu of the paid advertisements common to mainstream magazines, *Adbusters* intersperses its written and graphic content with parody antiads akin to social marketing on behalf of public-service and nonprofit organizations.[49] Recently there have been arguments against the validity and effectiveness of culture jamming. Some argue that culture jamming is easily co-opted and commodified by the market, which tends to defuse its potential for consumer resistance.[50] Others posit that the culture-jamming strategy of rhetorical sabotage, used by *Adbusters*, is easily incorporated and appropriated by clever advertising agencies and thus is not a very powerful means of social change.[51]

The retail industry and many major brands come under attack from the arts in a variety of ways. One of the most popular and now well-known fringe activities are the comic performances of Reverend Billy and the Church of Life After Shopping.[52] The reverend says on his Facebook page,

> Reverend Billy and the Life After Shopping Gospel Choir believe that Consumerism is overwhelming our lives. The corporations want us to have experiences only through their products. Our neighborhoods, "commons" places like stoops and parks and streets and libraries, are disappearing into the corporatized world of big boxes and chain stores. But if we "back away from the product"— even a little bit, well then we Put The Odd Back In God!
>
> The supermodels fly away and we're left with our original sensuality. So we are singing and preaching for local economies and real—not mediated through products—experience.
>
> We like independent shops where you know the person behind the counter or at least you like them enough to share a story. We ask that local activists who are defending themselves against supermalls, nuke plants, gentrification—call us and we'll come and put on our "Fabulous Worship!"[53]

Antiwaste

Research has shown just how much food is tossed into the trash of homes across America. A study conducted by University of Arizona academic Timothy Jones, suggests that up to 50% of all food ready for harvest is wasted, with wastage occurring at all stages including the farms and orchards where food is grown, the warehouses where food is stored, retail outlets where food is sold, and the dining rooms where food is eaten, with vast quantities ending up in landfills.[54] This study found that not only is edible food discarded that could feed people who need it, but also the rate of loss could save consumers and corporations tens of billions of dollars each year. On average, households waste 14% of their food purchases. Of that, 15% includes products still within their expiration date but never opened. It is the recognition of this behavior, and a desire to rectify the situation, that drives people to dumpster dive as opposed to put food on the table per se.

Dumpster diving is one fringe consumer response to directly mitigate the effect of food wastage. The practice, also known as freeganism, skipping, or containering, involves sifting through trash to find items that have been discarded by their owners that may be useful to the dumpster diver—for instance, flour disposed of by a restaurant that is fine for consumption in another setting. While dumpster diving may once have been the pastime of squatters or the hard up, it has spawned in practice and it is not solely about necessity in today's society. Rather, this behavior is about an ideology in the search for things that other people have thrown out that are still useful, can be eaten or recycled, and have residual value. This practice goes beyond the rummaging of inorganic rubbish collections that occurs, for instance, on the streets of capital cities. These consumers are prepared to climb into dumpsters or bins at apartment buildings and behind shopping centers, often under cover of darkness (and under the threat of criminal charges), in an attempt to reclaim wasted items suitable for further consumption. This behavior suggests that one's rubbish can also be considered another's treasure. Take Judy, an early thirtysomething dumpster diver and who works a day job in a restaurant and earns a reasonable salary. She can afford to put food on her table, but about once a week she will head out, armed with protective gloves and a torch to scavenge. She has certain places where she will frequent and looks for food where the sell-by date has only just expired or food that is edible but where the packaging has been damaged (often disposed of because it is substandard only in the eye of the shopper). Judy's behavior highlights not only the residual value of disposed goods by others, but also the ease with which people freely dispose of products.

Antiglobalization

The antiglobalization movement has arisen in opposition to corporate globalization, the process by which multinational corporations move their operations overseas with the intention of lowering their costs and increasing profits. It is the process by which cost reduction is achieved that is concern for the antiglobalization movement, from the perceived neoimperialist actions of big business to the exploitation of developing nations. The exploitation of developing nations is a central tenet of author and social activist Naomi Klein's book *No Logo*,[55] which discusses the detrimental effects of globalization on society. Klein explains how participants base their criticisms on a number of related ideas, such as an opposition to large, multinational corporations having unregulated political power and to the powers exercised through trade agreements and deregulated financial markets. Specifically, corporations are accused of seeking to maximize profit at the expense of sabotaging work-safety conditions and standards; labor hiring and compensation standards; environmental conservation principles; and the integrity of national legislative authority, independence, and sovereignty. Sweatshops remain a potent symbol of the downside of globalization in our consumer society, and recent years have seen several steps by governments, including the Central America Free Trade Agreement (CAFTA) in 2005.

Numerous global brands come under the microscope from anti-global protestors and high profile events such as the "McLibel" trial in the case the McDonald's fast-food chain. The trial, in the British court, between McDonald's and Helen Steel and Dave Morris (a former postman and a gardener from London), ran for 2½ years and became the longest ever English trial. The defendants were denied legal aid and their right to a jury, so the whole trial was heard by a single Judge, Mr. Justice Bell. He delivered his verdict in June 1997. The verdict was devastating for McDonald's. The judge ruled that they exploit children with their advertising, produce misleading advertising, are culpably responsible for cruelty to animals, are antipathetic to unionization, and pay their workers low wages. The message for retailers from this case is that no business, even a giant like McDonald's, is immune from the forces of active customer rebellion.

Antisweatshop

The U.S. Government Accountability Office defines a sweatshop as an employer that violates more than one federal or state labor law governing minimum wage and overtime, child labor, industrial homework, occupational safety and health, worker's compensation, or industry regulation. Sweatshops have been on the rise since the early 1970s; however, it was during the 1990s that human rights and antisweatshop activists increased their efforts to improve working conditions and raise wages for workers in developing countries. Between 1990 and 1996, the number of articles in major newspapers about sweatshop and child labor activities more than tripled. Major campaigns against large footwear companies such as Nike forced these firms to raise wages, improve working conditions for their workers, and sign codes of conduct.[56] Sweatshops exist both internationally and domestically, and the U.S. Department of Labor estimates that over 50% of sewing shops in the United States are sweatshops as defined in using the previous definition.

Various groups support the antisweatshop movement today. The U.S. National Labor Committee brought sweatshops into the mainstream media in the 1990s when it exposed the use of sweatshop and child labor to sew Kathie Lee Gifford's Walmart label. The International Labor Rights Fund filed a lawsuit[57] on behalf of workers in China, Nicaragua, Swaziland, Indonesia, and Bangladesh against Walmart charging the company with knowingly developing purchasing policies particularly relating to price and delivery time that are impossible to meet while following the Walmart code of conduct. Labor unions have helped support the antisweatshop movement out of concern both for the welfare of people in the developing world and that companies will move jobs from the United States to elsewhere in order to capitalize on lower costs.

It is important to note that the antisweatshop movement has much in common with the antiglobalization movement. Both consider sweatshops harmful, and both have accused many companies (such as the Walt Disney Company, The Gap, and Nike) of using sweatshops. The movement argues that there tends to be a race to the bottom, as multinationals leap from one low-wage country to another searching for lower production costs.

Anti–Chain Store

Independent retailers and consumers (predominantly women) have been known to display anti–chain store reactions in response to the expansion of large retail chains. These reactions first arose in the United States in response to the expansion of big retail chains in the 1920s and 1930s. Daniel Scroop, historian and author of the book *Mr. Democrat: Jim Farley, the New Deal, and the Making of Modern American Politics*, has traced the history of the anti–chain store consumer movement in America. According to Scroop, chain stores have reduced the aesthetic appeal of America's main streets; they have imperiled the livelihoods of local merchants and contributed to the erosion of the national character. This movement is similar to the antiglobalization protests of the 1990s and 2000s and has been said to be "a constitutive element of the modern politics of consumption in the United States."[58]

In another article, *The Anti-Chain Store Movement and the Politics of Consumption*, Scroop discussed the advent of chain store taxes and subsequent state laws as "the most concrete achievement of the great wave of anti-chain store protest."[59] Through a very detailed account of the antichain movement throughout American national history, Scroop also argues that the Depression-era and anti–chain store movement was the same as its modern-day counterpart. In the 1920s and 1930s, small retailers themselves formed the core of the movement. While it is true that small retailers, joined by an assortment of community activists, have persistently challenged big-box retailers at the local level over the last 20 years or so, today consumer activist groups and unions are proving to be the most forceful and effective opponents of the big chains.

Since the 1980s, small retailers in numerous communities across the United States have combined at the local level with small-town preservationists and an assortment of community activists to form coalitions opposed to the rise of big-box retail. In the 1990s, campaigns against big-box stores such as Walmart resurfaced similar anti–chain store politics in the United States. This is exemplified on the shelves of U.S. bookstores, where guidebooks advising retailers and others on how to keep big-box stores out of their communities mingle with popular polemics seeking to exploit the widespread public unease over the power of corporate retail in general and of Walmart in particular. This situation has been further impacted in recent years by ever-increasing globalization and the global financial crisis.

Many people are instinctually abandoning their patronage of big-box department and grocery stores like Costco, Home Depot, and Kmart with their foreign and Wall Street ownership in favor of returning their business to small- to medium-sized stores. These store types emphasize personal contact and service for the customer, which the megastore, corporate-profit-center model cannot provide but only talk about in its advertising. Other advantages of smaller businesses are their local own-ership and the retention and recycling of both profits and taxes in the community in which workers and owners live. The superficial savings alleged in the purchase of the often large quantities of frivolous things from the big box stores are more than negated by money going to distant corporations and investors that actively destroy as many middle-class-sustaining jobs as possible for the greatest profits, the loss of local control, the importation of taxpayer-subsidized cheap labor, disregard for local decision making, and lack of responsiveness to the community.

An additional advantage of smaller scale retailing is that the mer-chants can be more flexible and stock products made regionally, the value of which is based on inherent excellence, environmentally benign design, and word-of-mouth reputation, rather than expensive advertising cam-paigns that hype the image of mediocre lowest-common-denominator branded products made for a world market in the most exploitive factory available at the time.[60]

Antitechnology

It is difficult to argue against the fact that rapid advancements in com-puter technology during the last half of this century have changed almost every facet of life. However, dating back to the early 19th century, the Luddites have been a social movement opposed to industrialization, automation, computerization, and new technologies,[61] which they fear will leave them without work and is a threat to overall livelihood. The movement began in Nottingham in 1811 as part of the British Indus-trial Revolution and spread rapidly throughout England thereafter. It is important here to note the emergence of the Luddite fallacy—the idea (generally accepted by economists) that technological progress will never lead to massive, long-term unemployment. The reasoning here is as labor-saving technologies improve, some workers will lose their jobs in the short-term but production also becomes more efficient, leading to lower prices for the goods and services produced, and that, in turn, leaves consumers with more money to spend on other things. One of the most extreme historical examples of this is the mechanization of agriculture in the United States, where (in the late 1800s) about three quarters of U.S. workers were employed in agriculture; today the number is around 3%.

Instead of long-term structural unemployment, affected workers were absorbed by other industries, and average wages and overall prosperity increased dramatically.[62]

In response to the undercurrent of fear regarding technological advancements, the related term "technophobia" has emerged, which means the fear or dislike of advanced technology or complex devices, especially computers. It is exemplified in popular culture and thinking through movies such as *Blade Runner* and the story of *Frankenstein*. Most real-life examples are far more sedate, running from fear of learning to use a computer to opting to withdraw cash at a live bank teller rather than an ATM. Several groups are often said to be technophobic: most notably the Luddites,[63] but also the Amish and, more recently, businesses and environmentalist groups trying to prevent the spread of technology. One study, published in the journal *Computers in Human Behavior* was conducted between 1992 and 1994 and assessed people's level of technological sophistication and level of technophobia across 23 countries.[64] Of the 3,392 respondents, 29% reported high-level technophobic fears, with several differences across countries (Japan: 58%; India: 82%; Mexico: 53%). In his 2002 article in *Forbes*, popular American editor and columnist Dan Seligman discerns four possible reasons for modern day technophobia.[65] First, new technology threaten the material interests of some groups; second, new technology is thought to be unhealthy; third, new technologies are resisted because they are viewed, correctly, as fostering economic growth, and growth is viewed, incorrectly, as bad for the human species; and fourth, technology is said to offend religious faith.

Consumer resistance to technology can have particular impacts on retailers, particularly those that operate online given some consumers mistrust in the channel (and technology).

Part II Summary

In part II of the book, we developed a visual representation of consumer resistance, or the forces that combine together to lead the consumer to act in a resistant manner.

Macro and micro forces can combine in such a way that when a conflict occurs, the consumer can be driven to resistance, which can manifest in one of many mainstream or fringe activities.

While fringe activities may, or may not, directly impact retailers in today's climate, these activities are important to understand and follow; they are areas where consumer resistance is occurring, and as such it is important for all business, including retail, to understand. In this chapter we have stressed that the range of individual and collective behaviors are vast and can be private or public displays, both having a potential impact on the retail bottom line. In the final chapters, we analyze what strategies retailers are employing to manage consumer resistance and cater to the inscrutable shopper.

PART III

The Strategic Retailer

Although hotly debatable in the global media, poor economic conditions also provide retailers with distinct opportunities. For instance, some retailers develop innovative strategies around offering cash or trade-in exchange for unwanted electronics and gold (e.g., mygoldparty.com). Amazon offers consumers gift cards in exchange for secondhand video games. To be eligible, games must be in good condition and include the original manual, cover art, and case. Amazon's video game trade-in site lists a wide variety of games it will accept, along with their trade-in values. Furthermore, for shipments valued at US$10 or more, Amazon even gives consumers a way to ship them for free. On receipt, Amazon deposits an Amazon.com gift card into the consumer's account, and the purchase cycle can begin again.

Future retailing success will depend on understanding and reacting to the rapidly emerging and changing characteristics of customers, such as those based on the economy and finances, but also in terms of their potential for mainstream or fringe resistance. Essentially, the most successful retailers of tomorrow are adapting to customer behavior by understanding who their customers are, what they look like, what they want, and how and why they are changing.

A key to retail success is an understanding of the customer based on current and relevant data collection and analysis.

We are regularly told that UK retailer Tesco, and specifically their Clubcard program, is considered as a best practice example of this. In the face of downbeat trading during the credit crunch, Tesco did what it has always been good at and reacted quickly to a changing market by using its Clubcard data to send out targeted offers to customers. This essential information on actual buying behavior has guided most of the key decisions that Tesco's management team has taken in recent years (such as the launch of Tesco.com and its financial services arm, as well as its entry into nonfood categories such as clothing). Tesco has also begun profiling and targeting customers using this data, which ranks customers' enthusiasm for promotions and brand loyalty.[1]

In part III we take on a macro, global retail perspective and discuss some of the key implications for retailers that arise from consumer resistance in retail. Further, we discuss what some of the world's most strategic retailers are doing in terms of being responsible, which in turn is having a positive effect on inscrutable shoppers worldwide. We integrate our learning from the many discussions we have had with senior retailers across the globe, in which we consistently learn that those who fully understand their customers are harnessing the power of customer data. This could be in the form of data mining from an existing database of customers, developing insight by scanning data at the point of purchase, monitoring the conversations of online communities relevant to the brand or category, or collecting primary data by way of market research about *their* customers, including how they act, what they want, and what makes them purchase. Such data allows retailers to be more customer-centric and therefore more flexible in tailoring offers and responding to the changing needs and preferences of valuable customers, and the market in general. The primary benefits of using and understanding customer data within retail is often discussed in terms of data's ability to target and reward shoppers, potentially leading to an increase in foot traffic, higher conversion rates, increased loyalty and satisfaction, and larger basket size.

CHAPTER 6

Implications for Retailers

A business is confronted with a plethora of different propositions that it may want to communicate as its core credentials, for instance a discount offer, a high-fashion offer, limited offer, or a range of green, or sustainable propositions—not to mention the range of environmental, social, and economic strategies it might employ in its drive to be a good corporate citizen. As we have shown throughout this book, there are many terms that can be used, sometimes interchangeably, to convey that a company is trying to play its role as corporate citizen. For the purpose of this chapter, we will call all the possible terms that a company may wish to communicate about being a good corporate citizen "green credentials." Green credentials can be a powerful marketing tool, with companies increasingly using such claims to market their brand and differentiate themselves, and their products, from the competition. The ultimate payoff for business is that many consumers consider these green claims a major factor in choosing which brands to buy, where to shop, and how to evaluate products. This reinforces the need for accurate information in order for consumers to make informed decisions. For instance, The Body Shop, as it is with many companies, is communicating its green credentials to consumers, which is an effective strategy to increase sales, given that experts at the Food Marketing Institute's Sustainability Summit agree that educating consumers about the social responsibilities involved with products helps to boost sales.

For most consumers, sustainable considerations are an important tie-breaker when deciding between two otherwise equal products, and they are a driver in product switching. However, it is not enough to just put green products on the shelf; consumers need to be better educated about products, and leveraging in-store communication can assist in making the sale. What many companies do not consider is that they face the risk of greenwashing in communicating their green credentials in the market.

Greenwashing refers to the act of misleading consumers regarding the environmental practices of a company or the environmental benefits of a product or service, as well as the absence of legally binding regulations. Today, many companies are struggling to find the most effective way to pitch their green credentials without sounding insincere, opportunistic, or like just another marketing ploy. In this chapter, we discuss the importance of communicating sustainable credentials to educate consumers and to provide business transparency. In addition, we discuss the risk of greenwashing, a major issue for all businesses to consider.

The Need for Education

Whenever we speak to consumers, they consistently have one key message: businesses need to educate them on what they can do (e.g., the products that a company sells) to become more environmentally friendly in their lives, households, and workplaces. Consumers are often confused by, and therefore struggle to interpret green claims; they just do not know what to do or how to engage in everyday consumption (and their lifestyle more broadly) in a green manner. This can be attributed not only to the complex nature of sustainability issues, but also to the corporate marketing efforts over the last decade. Global oil and gas company BP, for example, has attempted to overhaul its image to be seen as environmentally friendly brand. Often BP advertisements show solar panels, windmills, and waving fields of grass with no reference to the oil trade. The change in name from British Petroleum to BP, the green sun logo, and the new slogan "Beyond Petroleum" attempted to present the brand as environmentally friendly even though BP only invested a very small fraction of its profits in alternative energy in 2009. According to a 2007 green brands survey, the general public perceived BP as more green than any of the other petroleum companies, and it was at the top of a list of companies that had become more green in the previous 5 years.[2] Unfortunately, when the company's Deepwater Horizon offshore well began leaking tens of thousands of barrels of crude oil into the Gulf of Mexico, the company's environmental credibility was destroyed, as it pointed to the fact that BP still derived more than 99% of its revenues from gas and petroleum.[3]

Research highlights the need for better retail and shopper marketing programs to close the consumer education gap. For instance, according to a recent study by the Grocery Manufacturers Association (GMA) and Deloitte, there is a large market open to considering green products (95% of those surveyed); however, only about a fifth of shoppers purchase green products.[4] At times, concerns about product performance and credibility of the environmental claims are the reasons shoppers opt not to buy green products, but more often communication and product education are the primary obstacles.[5] A lack of knowledge about green products was identified as a roadblock for green purchase behavior by Boston Consulting Group in a 2008 study titled "Capturing the Green Advantage for Consumer Companies."[6] The authors discuss two main obstacles in green consumer behavior: The first is awareness, as consumers are often unaware of green alternatives in many categories, let alone the benefits of green products. The second is the perception of a lack of choice in the market, as consumers see only a limited number of green products available in stores.

The Need for Transparency

In a world of increasingly proactive, demanding, cynical, and resistant customers, there is a genuine business requirement to be transparent because details of policies, practices, and finances are largely in the public domain. Transparency, like charity, starts in the home, and retailers need to work on the internal processes and procedures through the supply chain to the sale of their products, including consumption and disposal. The shift toward transparency requires companies to focus on suppliers, affinity partners, customers, and investors. Business transparency is therefore more than a corporate social responsibility policy, and it needs to extend beyond an individual brand or product to every element of retail. These final two stages of a products life cycle, consumption and disposal, are important because customers can be educated about how they can be more sustainable in their own lives.

Retailers (like many other businesses) are facing increasing pressure to measure and report on their carbon footprint. The full footprint of a retail organization encompasses a wide range of emission sources from direct use of fuels to indirect impacts such as employee travel or emissions from related organizations up and down the supply chain. According to a 2009 Corporate Sustainability and Responsibility International (CSRI) global report, 76% of companies are consistently implementing or planning their carbon management strategies, while 60% actively measured their carbon footprint. U.S. companies had the lowest levels of carbon monitoring, with only 54% measuring their footprint, compared with 92% of Australasian respondents and 62% of European respondents. The report, based on a survey of over 300 companies across various industries, looked at how companies are integrating greenhouse gas management into their overall business strategy. Companies showed a strong interest in carbon offsetting with more than "two thirds claiming they have already bought offsets or would consider doing so before 2012[7]." With or without a specific carbon management strategy, nearly all companies were implementing energy-efficiency measures (85%), recycling activities (79%), and waste-reduction initiatives (68%).[8]

Environmental concerns and consumer demand for green products are the driving forces behind the need for, and growth of, green communications. Green communications aim to achieve a balance between the objectives of sales and profits and the concern for society and the environment. Thus green marketing can be defined as the holistic management process responsible for identifying, anticipating, and satisfying the needs of customers and society in a profitable and sustainable way. Such attention on the environment has been manifested in two ways: First, the public has become more aware of the need for environmental considerations, and second, companies are becoming increasingly environmentally responsible and using green marketing activities. This increase in environmental consciousness and concern is a good incentive for marketing decision makers to adopt new and more consistent practices.

However, consumers have become increasingly closed off from genuine environmental messages. This is the result of customers' increasing scrutiny toward green claims, as well as the damage caused by overstated green claims. The 2008 Green Gap Survey[9] looked into the perception of green marketing among 1,080 adults. When respondents saw a product advertised as green or environmentally friendly, 48% believed this to mean that the product has a positive impact on the environment. But when respondents were questioned on their beliefs about the environmental messaging, 90% said that companies must not only say a product or service is good for the environment but also prove such claims. Of those surveyed, 73% were more skeptical, believing companies that communicate about the environment are doing it to try to sell more products or services. A further

52% were just overwhelmed by the number of environmental messages and could not make a judgment either way. Despite these findings, sustainability communications can influence consumer behavior. Global market insight and information group TNS conducted a study of 13,128 people across 17 countries analyzing green attitudes, perceptions, and behaviors in 2008.[10] They report that for 24% of respondents, green messages have a "significant or large influence." However, the range of responses across particular countries is noticeably wide. The research asked consumers if a company that promoted itself as green influenced their purchasing decisions. In terms of the global average, 24% of respondents said this has a significant or large influence; again, the range of responses across countries was wide. Consumers in the United States and the United Kingdom said they were influenced to a limited extent, with only 19% and 17%, respectively, saying green claims have a "significant or large influence." Five distinct emerging markets occupied the top of the table: Brazil (58%), Mexico (49%), Argentina (42%), Thailand (42%), and Malaysia (35%).

Jacquelyn Ottman, Edwin Stafford, and Cathy Hartman, professors of marketing from Utah State University suggest that, in order to appeal credible, successful green marketing must satisfy two objectives: environmental quality and customer satisfaction.[11] Misjudging either can be termed "green marketing myopia," the common pitfall of companies' tunnel vision. This term is borrowed from Theodore Levitt's 1960 concept "marketing myopia," discussed in a seminal *Harvard Business Review* article, and still studied by business students today.[12] In this article, he characterized the common pitfall of companies' tunnel vision on "managing products" (i.e., product features, functions, and efficient production) rather than "meeting customers' needs" (i.e., adapting to consumer expectations and anticipation of future desires). The risk of environmental marketing failure is high because consumers select products and new innovations that offer benefits they desire. Research indicates that many green products have failed because marketers focus on their products' greenness over the broader expectations of consumers. The diversity and availability of green products indicate that consumers are not indifferent to the value offered by environmental benefits. For example, the market growth of organic foods and energy-efficient appliances lies in consumer desire for perceived safety and money savings, respectively.

The Risk of Greenwashing

No doubt, brands around the world have made major strides in enacting eco-friendly initiatives. However, those businesses and brands that greenwash are actively coming under attack by consumers themselves, consumer-protection bodies, and relevant nongovernmental organizations.

The term "greenwashing" refers to the act of misleading consumers regarding the environmental practices of a company or the environmental benefits of a product or service, as well as the absence of legally binding regulations. Often the reasons that organizations are tempted to greenwash are due to internal inconsistencies; often organizational departments work in silos, or the environmental message is borne out of just one department and therefore fails to thrive across all business departments. The recent economic downturn has also highlighted that some organizations adopt green practices only when short-term savings can be made and a long-term view of the issue is often overlooked.

The Whole Foods supermarket chain in the United States has been publically identified as a retailer guilty of a greenwashing claim with regard to its plastic bag policy. In early 2008, the Whole Foods supermarket chain launched a well-publicized program aimed at phasing out plastic bags, focusing its campaign on the slogan of "paper good, plastic bad." However, in terms of being environmentally friendly, plastic bags beat paper bags on almost every measure. For instance, making paper bags creates five times as much solid waste and 50 times as much water pollution. Furthermore, the production of plastic bags consumes approximately 40% less energy. Complaints regarding false advertising have been made against Whole Foods, which highlights the importance of ensuring that when it comes to the environment, misleading consumers is a serious issue.[13] In another recent study released by consumer rights magazine, *Which?*, a number of household-name retailers, including Tesco, Sainsbury's, and Ecover, failed to adequately substantiate the claims made on green product labels.[14] The study examined 14 cleaning products and concluded that almost half of the "eco" laundry tablets, toilet cleaners, and diapers analyzed made claims that the companies could not support with adequate evidence. In particular, the study found that each of the toilet cleaners it scrutinized from Tesco, Sainsbury's, Ecover, and Green Force made at least one green claim that was not backed up by evidence from the manufacturer. Sainsbury's defended its labeling, arguing that the product is verified by the European Union Ecolabel, which offers independent assurance of a product's environmental credentials.

Consumer research has highlighted a gap between companies' aspirations and their actions, and there is some skepticism about companies' apparent good intentions. A study of 1,018 products in six category-leading big box stores in North America by TerraChoice Environmental Marketing Inc. found that almost all stores were guilty of some form of greenwashing. The information was not necessarily false, but in many cases, the retailers withheld the truth.[15] From this research, TerraChoice has developed "six sins" of greenwashing: The first sin is hidden trade-offs, which suggest a product is green based on a single environmental attribute or an unreasonably narrow set of attributes. The second sin is having no proof, which is stating any environmental claim that cannot be substantiated by easily accessible supporting information or by a reliable third-party certification. The third sin is vagueness, which, for instance, could be a claim so poorly defined or broad that its meaning is likely to be misunderstood. The fourth sin is irrelevance, committed by making an environmental claim that may be truthful but is unimportant and unhelpful for consumers seeking environmentally preferable products. The fifth is the lesser of two evils, or claims that may be true within the product category but risk distracting the consumer from the greater environmental impacts of the category as a whole. The last sin is distorting the truth, which is committed by making environmental claims that are simply false.

CHAPTER 7

Responsible Retailing

In today's interconnected global economy, the long-term value and success of business are inextricably linked to sustainability and the integration of environmental, social, and governance issues into corporate management and operations. Sustainability is a complex issue and impacts all business functions, in all regions, and is notoriously difficult to manage and define. According to a report released by consulting group The Hartman Group, consumer awareness of "sustainability" as a term, as well as a way of life, is growing. Changing attitudes and behaviors are reflected in consumption patterns, signaling the "increasing desire among consumers to live more responsibly."[1] According to the UN, the definition of sustainability is "meeting humanities needs today, without endangering future generations."[2] The scope includes environmental, social, and governance areas across economic, physical, and political boundaries.

By definition, a sustainable business is any organization that participates in environmentally friendly or green activities to ensure that all processes, products, and manufacturing activities adequately address current environmental concerns while maintaining a profit.

A sustainable business is one that strives to meet the triple bottom line and generally meets the following four criteria:

1. Incorporates principles of sustainability into each of its business decisions.
2. Supplies environmentally friendly products or services that replace demand for nongreen products or services.
3. Is greener than its traditional competition.
4. Has made an enduring commitment to environmental principles in its business operations.

In this chapter we outline some of the major initiatives being rolled out in a bid to be more sustainable in business. First, we briefly discuss corporate social responsibility.

Corporate Social Responsibility

Corporate social responsibility (CSR) is the act of ensuring that business operations do not adversely impact society's calls for a push toward ethics in business practice. Traditionally, CSR was a focus of the government, but increasingly retailers are at the forefront of social campaigns. The emergence of nonfinancial reporting has also increased the transparency of corporate actions.[3] Businesses not only are increasingly performing self-audits but also are performing a social compliance audit on suppliers. These audits ensure that suppliers are adhering to minimum standards in employee safety, work practices, child labor practices, and fair wages. This type of system is particularly directed toward overseas suppliers and ensuring that they positively cooperate is a business challenge.

Organizations are also beginning to look at ethics with regard to their buying practices to ensure no undue pressure is placed on suppliers in terms of pricing or that buyers are not accepting bribes and gifts in exchange for trading terms, which has been the case for French hypermarket retailer Carrefour in China. In this instance, eight management-level employees were arrested for taking bribes at the city's procurement center and in seven other outlets. The importance of social compliance for retailers ultimately lies in how the consumer will perceive the brand as a whole. Not surprisingly, reports of unethical situations have been shown to damage the brand reputation of the retailer, and accordingly, reports of sound social compliance can enhance brand image.

Carbon Footprinting

Retailers, as well as many other businesses and industries, are increasingly facing pressure to measure and report on their carbon footprint. The full footprint of a retail organization encompasses a wide range of emission sources from direct use of fuels to indirect impacts such as employee travel or emissions from related organizations up and down the supply chain. As was discussed in Chapter 6, much variation exists across industry sectors and countries in terms of the degree to which organizations are integrating carbon management strategies into the broader business.

UK clothing and food retailer, Marks & Spenser (M&S) actively measures its carbon footprint across three areas: customers, suppliers, and company operations. In doing so, and via its *How We Do Business* report, M&S charts the progress the company has made in its 100 "Plan A" sustainability commitments.[4] Since the inception of Plan A in 2007, M&S has successfully reduced total carbon emissions by 8 %; reduced store refrigeration emissions by 18 %; increased the efficiency of its fleets by 30 %; increased recycling rates for operations waste to 88 %, and reduced use of food carrier bags by 83 %.[5] Marks & Spencer's initiatives have achieved a 20 % reduction in food packaging, increased energy efficiency, and (most importantly) invested over £50 million (US$ 82 million) of profit from its Plan A activities back into the business. At the 3-year mark since the inception of Plan A, 62 of the original 100 commitments have been achieved, 30 were on plan to be achieved by 2012, and only 7 were behind schedule.

Retail Facilities

Sustainable facility development is often at the forefront of environmental planning as it physically signifies an organization's environmental activities and footprint. Environmental design seeks to reduce the use of non-renewable resources and enhance the use of renewable resources and recycled content while minimizing impact on the environment.[6] Savvy retailers have taken on the challenge of incorporating sustainable development principles and practices into the design of company facilities, from eco-friendly materials to heating, ventilation, and air-conditioning (HVAC) systems that have a low impact on the environment.[7] Tesco, Carrefour, and Walmart are doing just this and are currently in the process of opening a range of new energy-saving stores.

In response to the increasing number of commercial businesses greening their operations, national green building standards are being established around the world, most notably in the United States with the U.S. Green Building Council's (USGBC) Leadership in Energy and Environmental Design (LEED) green building rating system. The program is aimed at evaluating the sustainability of green buildings and is impacting the way commercial and residential properties are being designed, built, and operated, with retailers and shopping centers striving to attain this accreditation.[8] The LEED rating system awards credit points to green buildings, including retail interiors, based on sustainable sites, energy and atmosphere, water efficiency, indoor environmental quality, materials and resources, and innovation in design. If a building scores the required number of points, it achieves one of four progressive levels of certification: basic, silver, gold, and platinum.[9] The most recent version of the LEED system was launched in April, 2009. The third version builds on the fundamental rating system while providing a new structure for making sure the rating system "incorporates new technology and addresses the most urgent priorities like energy use and CO2 emissions."[10]

The Supply Chain

Green supply chains not only seek to reduce environmental impacts but also improve the overall strength, efficiency, and productivity of supply chain operations. Organizations have become increasingly aware of the propensity for environmental pollution incidents within their supply network to cost them in penalties, cleanup, and consumer backlash. As a result, minimum standards of environmental performance have become increasingly prevalent in the purchasing contracts and guidelines of multinational corporations for their local and global suppliers.[11] Companies are therefore increasingly looking for new approaches to manage carbon effectively, from sourcing and production, to distribution and product afterlife. In fact, one-third of the organizations surveyed by IBM Canada's Supply Chain Management Practice say they have already been asked by their trading partners to become much more green by incorporating CO_2 reduction into the overall supply chain management strategy.[12] A company not only can reduce its environmental emissions footprint but also can strengthen the brand image and develop a competitive advantage.

It is generally perceived that green supply chain management promotes efficiency and synergy among business partners and their lead corporations and helps to enhance environmental performance, minimize waste, and achieve cost savings. In 2005, a study by Purba Rao of the Asian Institute of Management in the Philippines and Diane Holt of Middlesex University in Dubai was one of the first empirical evaluations of the links among green supply chain management, increased competitiveness, and improved economic performance.[13] Their study identified that greening the different phases of the supply chain (both up and down) leads to an integrated green supply chain, which ultimately leads to enhanced competitiveness and economic performance. A 2009 survey of global chief supply chain officers by IBM found that while integration of sustainability principles increases complexity, a smarter and more sustainable supply chain can emerge as a "major business tool that can help control costs; manage risks and make profit in a fully responsible manner."[14] The research suggests that if a firm greens their supply chains, they not only achieve substantial cost savings in terms of improved efficiency, quality, and productivity improvement but also enhance sales, market share, and exploit new market opportunities to lead to greater profit margins. All of these contribute to the overall economic performance of the firm.

Product Life-Cycle Management

Manufacturers and retailers are also encouraged to consider product life-cycle management (PLM), with a focus on quality and durability that will stand the test of time as opposed to inexpensive, short-term fixes, as is commonly the case. PLM is the process of managing the entire life cycle of a product from its conception, through design and manufacture, to service and disposal. Well-documented benefits of this approach, such as reduced time to market, improved product quality, product optimization, reduced waste and efficiencies in product demand, and organizational integration, talk to the *waste-not mentality* discussed in consumer's mainstream minimization behaviors. In particular, the disposal stage (the final stage of consumption), is one area often overlooked by business.

With regard to recycling and disposal, retailers have an opportunity to respond to consumers' desire for product reuse prior to end disposal.

Again, M&S offers a great example of a retailer meeting environmental, social, and consumer pressures to reduce their waste to landfill by offering second-hand clothing items to the underprivileged and rewarding customers for their participation. As part of their plan and environmental sustainability pledge, M&S teamed up with Oxfam to encourage customers to recycle clothing items they no longer wear. As part of this program, customers are encouraged to donate M&S-labeled clothing items to

Oxfam and, in exchange, receive a voucher valued at £5 for use when they next spend £35 (the equivalent of a US$8 voucher for spending US$57) at an M&S store. The clothes-exchange program has been running since January 2008, has raised millions of pounds for Oxfam's charity work, and has since been extended to include the donation of M&S soft furnishings. As of late 2010, the M&S-Oxfam initiatives expanded again, along with UK fashion retailer Next, to trial a new recycling scheme that allows employees to donate clothing at offices and workplaces across the United Kingdom, which is then collected by the charity. This initiative is particularly important as Oxfam notes double-figure decreases in stock since the global financial crisis. Looking forward, an important consideration for retailers is their capability to develop new products and services that offer consumers the most convenience through the most appropriate channel. The M&S-Oxfam initiative demonstrates concern for the environment through recycling and concern for the greater community and charitable cause, as well as employee engagement in corporate social responsibility.

Product Sourcing

In the move toward becoming green, retail, wholesale, and manufacturing organizations are also ensuring that products are sourced from sustainable resources. Stemming from the concern for food transportation, there is also a growing trend among consumers demanding locally grown, organically raised produce and other food. Such trends are driven further by health concerns, a desire for better-tasting food, and an unease regarding environmental hazards. Increasingly consumers want key information to be displayed on their food, including country of origin, to enable more informed buying decisions. Consumers choose to buy local food options because it is good for the environment as it has not traveled a long distance. As one of the world's largest retailers, Walmart's produce travels an average 1,500 miles from farms to consumers' homes, with the retailer expecting to "save millions of food miles through local sourcing, better packing of its trucks, and improved logistics."[15]

The term "food miles" was coined in the mid-1990s in a report by the United Kingdom's SafeAlliance (now Sustain), which highlighted concerns over the negative environmental and socioeconomic impacts of increasing transport of food. Food miles are the distances traveled by foodstuffs from farm gate to consumer. The number of food miles has increased dramatically for several reasons, including to ensure out-of-season supply, to increase trade, to lower labor costs, to centralized packaging, and to allow for increased distance to shops. Sustain believes that more energy is put into transporting food long distances (in terms of nonrenewable fossil fuels) than is produced in the form of food calories. Environmentalists therefore warn of a huge pollution burden as a result of CO_2 emissions from the trucks and planes used to transport fresh food. Manufacturers such as Cadbury, Kellogg's, and General Mills have signed an industry pledge to create fewer and friendlier food transport miles, announced in 2008[16]. Companies, including Associated British Foods and Mars, have also signed a 10-point checklist to move toward a cut in the impact of domestic food transport on the environment in the United Kingdom. The pledge was signed through the United Kingdom's Food and Drink Federation and is a bid to meet a government-backed target of reducing the environmental and social impacts of food transport by 20% in 4 years compared to 2002 levels.

Beyond the issue of food miles, leading concerns in this area lie in organic and fair-trade products. Sales of organic food in Australia are estimated at around AU$500 million a year (the equivalent of US$530 million). The Fair Trade Association of Australia and New Zealand (FTA-ANZ) reports that the annual retail sales of fair-trade-certified products in Australia and New Zealand increased by almost 200% between 2009 and 2010 reaching almost AU$150 million (US$160 million). This growth is reflected in a global trend with worldwide fair-trade annual sales increasing by 15% as consumers spent an estimated US$5.7 billion fair-trade products globally.[17] As consumers demand transparency in many business areas, there is also a growing interest in a product's country of origin, with consumers increasingly patronizing stores that offer locally manufactured products.

Distribution

Producers, distributors, and retailers alike are also adopting environmentally friendly distribution systems. Concerned with limiting their carbon footprint, players at all levels of the retail industry are adopting energy-efficient distribution equipment and vehicles while reducing air transportation of goods. Tesco, for example, limits the air transportation of goods by sourcing the majority of products locally and regionally.[18] Tesco in the United Kingdom ensures its delivery trucks never leave a site empty and have been adapted to carry more stock on a second layer in the truck. Similarly, Walmart trucks do not use power when idling after the company installed auxiliary power systems to keep drivers comfortable while idling. These changes alone are saving the company US$277 million a year.[19] UK grocer Sainsbury's has received an award from the Energy Saving Trust for its commitment to eco-friendly product-delivery methods.

Although more environmentally friendly by nature compared to other transportation methods, there is a growing awareness of the need to minimize the environmental impact of transport via ship. Retailers who can incorporate environmentally conscious shipping choices, both to consumers and upstream to their supplier base, will not only reduce the costs of bringing a product to market but also differentiate themselves to consumers, strategic partners, and investors in a way that could provide a significant competitive advantage in the marketplace.[20] For example, in 2007, U.S. home-improvement goods retailer Lowe's increased its use of environmentally friendly carriers to 62 from only 4 in 2004 and increased its intermodal shipping by over 4,000 shipments. The company has also increased the use of full trailers and, since 2005, estimates this program has helped reduce carriers' highway travel by 500 million miles, resulting in savings of more than 100 million gallons in diesel fuels and 1 million tons of carbon.[21]

Waste Reduction

Businesses are under increasing pressure to reduce their own waste and packaging and to encourage consumers to recycle and reuse. Some governments are introducing laws governing the distribution of plastic bags, which often end up littering the countryside or going to landfill. In New Zealand for example, the New Zealand Retailers Association (NZRA) has taken steps to improve their bag-to-landfill situation after consumer research into plastic bag usage was commissioned. Based on these findings, the NZRA, in conjunction with the Packaging Council of New Zealand, launched the Make a Difference campaign. The campaign involves more than 600 participating supermarkets across the country focusing on the dispensing of plastic bags to encourage the use of eco-friendly bags or recycled bags. In 2009, the Packaging Council of New Zealand released data showing a 22% reduction in the number of plastic bags by shoppers over a 5-year period from August 2004 to July 2009, taking 157 million bags out of circulation.

In the absence of legislation, some retailers have taken matters into their own hands. French hypermarket Carrefour, for example, makes customers buy reusable plastic or nonwoven bags. Walmart has partnered with elementary schools in 12 U.S. states to give students an opportunity to recycle their household shopping and grocery bags through its Kids Recycling Challenge program. Schools are rewarded for each 60-gallon plastic collection bag brought to their local store. Around the world, retailers have made the switch to no bags at all or have begun to charge fees for plastic bags. In Australia, a major hardware chain, Bunnings, no longer provides bags but gives customers easy access to the cardboard boxes that the store has received with goods as a means to transport and carry goods.

In summary, retail businesses are able to implement several strategies to achieve growth and profitability while achieving more sustainable businesses overall.

Activities that contribute to a more sustainable business are of great interest to many customers who are looking for retailers and businesses to lead the way in improving society. The next chapter addresses a number of best practice learnings for retailers looking to address consumer resistance and incorporate sustainability into their operations: Best Practice Considerations.

CHAPTER 8

Best Practice Considerations

Edutainment

The impact of retail service encounters on customers has received considerable attention in academic and practitioner literature. In recent years, there has been increased emphasis on the notion of the retail experience. The in-store customer experience is a function of multiple sources of input from the environment and also one's own predisposition, expectations, motives, and past experience. Comparisons have been drawn between the principles of Gestalt psychology,[1] suggesting that customers perceive the retail environment as a whole. One of the best ways a brand can engage customers is to educate them on how to use the product. The role of education within a store is not exactly new, but what is increasingly happening is the blurring of education and entertainment. Education is characterized by the acquisition, or transfer, of knowledge from the store setting (through information cues and staff assistance) to the customer. For instance, customers within a store may be able to learn about how to use the product range in addressing their needs. The blending of entertainment and education stimulates high levels of excitement and fun within stores and offers a memorable experience for the customer.

Retailers are increasingly using this strategy to enhance their service offerings and to create a retail environment that is "different and special."[2] Retail executives in our research discussed the ways in which retailers will likely entertain, engage, and educate customers within the store environment, with a general belief this trend will continue into the future. In fact, some suggested the experiential retail environments will become more interactive using technology such as plasma televisions and kiosks to deliver educational material.

An extension to entertaining the customer within the store is to entertain children, allowing the parents to engage in the purchase process while children are otherwise occupied. Many retailers now include a children's playground as part of the store environment. KidZania[3] is a chain of theme parks where children can decide what they want to be when they grow up by actually doing the job. KidZania is a veritable city with an assortment of establishments covering the entire fabric of a working economy, from banks to hospitals, universities to salons, television stations to music lounges, and racetracks to supermarkets. Children can undertake over 70 professions including firefighters, chefs, engineers, models, actors, artists, radio hosts, photographers, television hosts, jewelry designers, police detectives, and mechanics among others. They are paid KidZos, the official currency of KidZania, for their services, which can be used to buy goods and services or even save in their bank account in KidZania, which provides them with an ATM card, too. Children function independently but are guided in each activity by Zoopervisors, the trained KidZania staff. KidZania Dubai spans over 80,000 square feet over two levels and is located in the entertainment precinct of the mall near Reel Cinemas, the 22-screen megaplex, and SEGA Republic, the largest indoor theme park of its kind in the Middle East. At KidZania, children are not only highly entertained but also educated through a real-life business and social environment. KidZania has won the Best Theme Park Worldwide Award from the Themed Entertainment Association in 2001, the International Association of Amusement Parks and Attractions (IAAPA) Top FECs of the World Award in 2006, the IAAPA Brass Ring Award for Industry Marketing in 2008, and most recently the Concept of the Year from MAPIC. The concept of KidZania, which blends fun with learning, has gained global appeal since its launch in Mexico in 1999. Today, the world has seven KidZania franchises. KidZania Cairo is Egypt's first edutainment center, expected to open in October 2012. It is the first KidZania in Africa, the second in the Middle East, and will span over 5,300 square meters. Once open, KidZania Cairo is expected to host up to 750,000 visitors annually, with the center offering a city for kids featuring an airport, a bank, a hospital, a department store for electronic appliances, in addition to a variety of food industries and restaurants.

Few retail formats have attracted as much attention and critical acclaim in recent years as Nike Town, particularly around its approach to themed retail and store edutainment.[4] Nike Town brand stores seamlessly blend sports-themed memorabilia and high-tech design to attract shoppers, and are as focused on selling the fitness lifestyle that Nike represents as much as the product it sells. Merchandise at Nike Town is grouped into different departments (called pavilions) that are classified by sport category, with care taken in the design and ambience of each pavilion so that it reflects the related sport. The running shoe department, for example, is set against a backdrop of light blue and white designed to echo a sky and clouds, and audio and video tools are also used to enhance the mood. In addition to entertaining consumers, Nike Town also educates them with strategically placed "inspiration boards" within the store, which detail the design and creation of various Nike products, from the original drawing and choice of materials to the rollout.

Edutainment as a retail strategy has great strength as it can eliminate much of the boredom of a predictable retail store. It can provide opportunity for further education on a wide range of topics relating to health, security, and community by including information on new products relevant to the customer's local community.

Differentiation

As globalization continues, differences across race, culture, and geography become secondary. Nowadays customers across the world are wearing the same labels, listening to the same music, watching the same advertisements, and often purchasing and or consuming the same products and services. Out of this has grown a perception of homogenization in retail and a subsequent desire for innovative and novel ideas, store concepts, and products in the market. The challenge is for retailers to increasingly differentiate their products to stand out from the crowd and grab the music retailing

One sector that is increasingly under threat and needing to reinvent and differentiate itself (from the online channel) is brick-and-mortar music retailers. In 2007, album sales in the United States plunged 9.5% compared with 2006, while sales of digital music tracks surged 45%.[5] However, it is debatable whether online music sales will end the presence of retailers of physical music recordings, as many customers still like to browse in stores. New Zealand music retailer, Real Groovy, has successfully focused on secondhand goods and imports secondhand material from the United States that would otherwise not be available in the local market.[6] While this retailer did experience financial trouble in 2009 as a result of increased competition, it is back on track and would appear to be successfully differentiating its offer from (new) music sales. In this section, we review some of the innovative ways in which retailers are differentiating themselves from the competition (e.g., through channels, cocreation, and service offerings).

Pomme Bébé (http://www.pommebebe.com) is a restaurant in Newport Beach, California, that serves nothing but organic baby and toddler meals prepared fresh in its on-site kitchen. Pomme Bébé peels, steams, and purees ingredients by hand, with the menu featuring seasonal recipes developed by five-star chef Laurent Brazier. Autumn dishes, for example, include apple cranberry puree, chicken pot pie blend, and autumn stew. With prices beginning at US$3.25 for a four-ounce serving, foods are also available online or through Whole Foods markets throughout the United States. What's especially interesting is that discerning baby clientele can sample Pomme Bébé's offerings—for free—at its onsite tasting bar and sit-down Bébé Lounge. The tasting bar resembles a sushi bar—featuring high chairs where the stools would be—with simple, clean lines to avoid distracting the pint-sized customers. The Bébé Lounge, meanwhile, includes seating for parents and has reportedly come to serve as a local hotspot for play dates and parties.

Differentiation can relate to all parts of the retail offer including products, formats, mall layout, and store facilities, or even services. Take for instance, Australian department store chain Myer, which recently set out to differentiate itself based on store design. In doing so, Myer undertook a multimillion dollar transformation of its iconic flagship store in the center of Melbourne city. The new store features a state-of-the-art shopping environment, inspired by some of the world's leading retailers in London, New York, and Paris and offers an awe-inspiring glass-domed cultural center, featuring fine dining, fashion parades, and other events. The addition of hundreds of new and exclusive fashion brands; a private shopping suite for in-house stylists and personal shoppers to assist shopper decision making; fine wine and delicate matched food in a champagne bar; and environment-friendly features, such as water harvesting and extensive natural light and ventilation. Overall, the store offers a retail experience and a shopping environment that Australia has never seen before, and reinforces Myer's position as a world-class retail destination.

From a shopper's viewpoint, convenience is another way to differentiate the offer and appeal to today's time-pressed consumers. In this context, convenience means an increase in the number of tasks that can be accomplished during a single shopping trip and a reduction in the time required to shop. The contemporary mall or shopping center fulfills many criteria when considering shopping convenience. Previous studies have shown that convenience is key in the minds of consumers undertaking routine and regular shopping expeditions. These shopping trips are underpinned by utilitarian shopping motivations as opposed to more recreational and hedonistic shopping. Utilitarian shopping visits include those to grocery stores, post offices, and banks. One of the first major studies into what customers regard as convenience with regard to shopping at a mall was recently conducted in Australia.[7] The study provides an important and relevant framework for considering the attributes sought by customers in shopping centers and how these attributes contribute to the costs of patronage. The overarching finding of this research study is that convenience is a key element of success for shopping center patronage. Convenience, according to the research, is a combination of retail center attributes including one-stop shopping, proximity, trading hours, shopping services, enclosure, pedestrian areas, compact size, compact design, compatibility, concentration, parking availability, parking proximity, parking type, number of lanes, traffic controls, and public transport.

The author notes that the data was sourced from Australian consumers, and other nations may have different attributes or assign different priorities to attributes. For example, trading hours may be irrelevant in global districts with 24/7 trading available to consumers. Some customers will resist patronizing a center that does not fulfill the bulk of their requirements for that visit. Other customers may resist if the pedestrian areas are too crowded, if the center's tenant mix is confusing, or if it is too difficult to access or park in the center.

Think Local, Act Local

Related to the trend towards cocooning, consumers are seeking unique offers that have some form of personal meaning to them. Increasingly this desire is manifested in the need to slow down the pace of their lives to allow more time for reflection and rest and to take time to enjoy processes, such as growing foods and preparing meals to be savored at the table with family in the evening rather than eating takeout in the car on the way home or reheating takeout in the microwave.

Customers are seeking products from their immediate local environment. One of the best examples of ultralocal in retail is the world's biggest retailer, Walmart.[8] This global retailer giant is able to balance the requirements of its organization while providing stores that are local in their response to the need for value and their proximity and convenience. A study of Walmart's promotional flyers[9] revealed that the giant retailer was able to demonstrate the promise of significant savings on a wide range of merchandise. At the same time the "the text and illustrations in the flyer reflect a rich blend of family, community and national norms." The study suggests that the combination of savings and community presents a "subtly utopian, nostalgic hometown, a place rich in American mythology where citizens achieve a balance between economic and moral pursuits." The research concluded "the world's largest retailer is experienced as the neighborly, small town shopkeeper, thereby legitimating itself among its consumer constituency."

Some retailers are taking the notion of ultralocal quite literally. For instance, one UK retailer, Fortnum and Mason, has placed beehives on the roof of one of their stores, where customers can watch a webcam of the bees as they create honey, which is then sold in the store. This trend could evolve in a number of ways in the future, with technology and our imaginations being the only barriers. One of our respondents in an interview discussed how robotic technology could be deployed to create ultralocal, community-based vegetable stores: "We might see the food we need grown on the corner of the street where you can walk down and buy it, [therefore reducing] the carbon footprint of that product."[10]

Global trade has resulted in more products traveling ever-increasing distances from production to final consumption and disposal. This process has a direct impact on customer resistance globally, from customers' boycotting products that have traveled a long distance, to consciously supporting local businesses and food growers. Food miles are a major trend driving this form of resistance. While food miles simplistically mean the distance food travels from farm to customer, the term implies the impacts on the food system, such as energy use and contribution to climate change, dependence on fossil fuels, and traffic congestion, as well as social and economic impacts on rural communities and developing countries. New Zealand food products have often been targeted by overseas campaigns for low food miles to illustrate the long distance products travel to export markets such as Europe, North America, or Japan. This attention poses a potential risk to New Zealand exports, but often local sourcing is not always the most environmentally sound solution if more emissions are generated at other stages of the product life cycle than during transport.[11]

Channels

Retail distribution has entered a new era in which consumers expect to be able to access retailers anytime, wherever they are, and on their own terms. Although the concept of multichannel retailing has been around for a number of years, the recent pressure from customers to add an online presence has driven more retailers to become multichannel entities. This has resulted in not only a form of customer resistance that is impacting particular shopping channels but also an opportunity for retailers to meet and exceed customer expectations in this regard, and at a faster pace than competitors. The key differentiator here is to offer a reliable, efficient, and integrated multichannel offer. One extreme outcome is that the customers resist the retail store altogether in an attempt to eliminate the middleman. However, our research has found that retail executives do worry about cannibalization from stores. Underlying this fear was the notion that manufacturers may cut out the retailer and communicate directly with the customer. One respondent we interviewed about future trends in retail described iTunes as an example of this possible trend:

> There are tribes of customers globally, and it may mean that one day there is no need for stores, at least in some categories. Look at iTunes for instance; I mean you can buy all the music you want online. Eventually you may be able to buy music from the artists; they will not need to go through record companies and distribution channels because the technology is there for them to be able to manufacture and distribute. I think that this applies to authors

as well, with the ability to sell books directly to customers. You're already seeing websites where artists go direct to the end user. Fashion people may get to the stage that they want designers to create limited and special pieces, and the end may be that there are many less retailers. (China, 2009)

The Internet has played a significant role within the multichannel retail context. The popularity of the Internet lies largely in the immediacy and convenience it affords today's time-poor customers. Survey research conducted during 2008 by online-payment company PayPal found that the main reasons why customers shopped online were to get better value (68% of respondents), to avoid crowds (65%), to avoid lines (48%), and to have access to a wider range of products (46%).[12] Research has also shown that there is an emotive element to shopping online, such as the joy of finding the right thing at the right price, getting a cheaper deal than expected, or finding something unique.[13] As a result, purchasing via the Internet has grown over the past decade at a rate that outpaces that of traditional retail channels, up to four to five times higher in some cases. According to a global survey conducted in 2009 by Forrester Research, 154 million customers made purchases online, 4% more than in 2008, helping online retail trade to grow 11% to US$155 billion in sales (excluding travel)[14]. Looking toward 2014, online retail sales are forecasted to continue their long history of double-digit growth, with online retail sales in the United States (excluding travel) expected to reach US$249 billion. The growth of that channel will, in part, be predicated on the ability of the retail industry to provide a purchase environment that is secure and perceived by the customer to be low risk.

Consumers' quest to find products themselves readily and easily is largely facilitated by the online channel, which can be inexpensively and quickly integrated as part of a broader operational business model. Savvy retailers have recognized the value afforded by the online channel (largely convenience and speed), with some taking this one step further by allowing customers to trade used products with each other. For instance, online fashion retailer ASOS recently empowered the individuality and waste-not mentality of its customers and launched an extension to its website called ASOS Marketplace. A cross between eBay and street blogs, ASOS's virtual market allows customers to take a picture of themselves in an item, post the image, and resell it online. The marketplace is also environmentally friendly, as users are essentially recycling clothes that might have otherwise been thrown away. Since the launch of ASOS Marketplace, the retailer has seen significant increases in site traffic and pre-Christmas sales. As ASOS CEO Nick Robertson has said,

> This is an exciting extension to ASOS' existing customer offer which makes perfect sense in today's market. . . . This is a sellers' platform. Our sellers will shape its future. With this initiative we are able to offer both individual and corporate customers an additional channel to sell their fashion merchandise in an environment, and in front of a customer, that is all about fashion.[15]

Cocreation

Increasingly, customers are communicating and collaborating within online communities and using their collective wisdom to create products themselves. Cocreation is the practice of developing new systems, products, designs, or marketing through the collaboration of brands with customers outside of the organization. This process engages the customer from the outset, as opposed to personalization, which takes place after product basics are developed. Similar to the World of Web 2.0, the collective knowledge of the community is a resource that has largely been untapped by the retail industry and offers another valuable opportunity for differentiation. In recognition of this, savvy retailers have begun creating goods, services, and experiences in close cooperation with customers. As part of such strategies, retailers are rewarding customers for their input via contests and gifts, and some customers are receiving a share of the development based on their input, suggestions, design, or ideas.

Academics, Robert Kozinets, Andrea Hemetsberger, and Hope Schau, note that collective customer creativity is qualitatively distinct from individual customer creativity and suggest it occurs when social interactions trigger new interpretations and new discoveries that individual customers alone could not have otherwise generated[16]. In their article, the authors discuss a now-classic example of the phenomenon of crowd-sourcing: the Threadless concept (http://www.threadless

.com). Other crowd-sourced creations include sneaker brand *Ryz*, which sells high-top sneakers featuring graphic designs created and voted into production by customers. Shoe design is a popular co-created product category, and one that is not always crowd-sourced. For instance, one innovative Australian online women's shoe brand, Shoes of Prey, has very recently (and quickly) grown to become one of Australia's leading online retail players, winning several industry awards over the past few years (including Best New Online Retailer, Most Innovative Online Retailer, Best Online Retail Marketing Initiative, and Best Online Strategy). In retailing its shoes, Shoes of Prey brings its customers into the design process and allows custom designs, which are then hand-made and shipped direct to the customer. As part of this process, women can choose from thousands of combinations of colors and accessories and truly co-create their own personal shoe, unique to only them (all at an affordable price). Off the back of its success online, Shoes of Prey is now expanding internationally and exploring a move into offline retail, with a trial currently underway with Marui, a department store chain in Japan. After just over a month, the trial is tracking exceptionally well and will likely be rolled out into additional Marui stores. Shoes of Prey is also working on some very exciting visualization and customization technology that transfer particularly well into store-based retailing. This retail proposition around co-creation also meets consumer demand for differentiation, interactivity, and engagement, as well as breaking through the boredom customers often feel regarding retail and product offers.

Cocreation facilities for the customers directly address individual needs for identity through personalization. The cocreation process can also be highly entertaining, can be linked to local and virtual communities, and can give the store opportunities to inform and educate their customers while getting to understand their needs and wants in much more detail.

Service

Differentiation via service is not novel, but it does have a significant effect on the customer's perception of the experience, with exceptionally good service leading to flow on effects, such as positive word-of-mouth. Conversely, poor service can lead to negative word-of-mouth and, possibly consumer resistance movements such as boycotts. Research reveals that companies that offer poor service are being hit by boycotts and therefore damage to their reputation. According to a recent survey of 2,082 consumers by the UK government and politics portal for news and opinion, *YouGov*, 47% have boycotted a company that has let them down, while 77% share their bad experiences with family and friends. Some 47% file a complaint, and 26% post a review online. According to 22% of respondents, utility companies offer the worst customer service, followed by strip (versus mall) retailers selected by 21%. Staff talking to each other when a customer is waiting for assistance was the biggest irritant for 48% of respondents.[17]

As part of our interviews in recent years, retailers have brought the notion of premium service as a differentiator to our attention. Many have felt that service is an innovation that is largely difficult to replicate by competitors:

> Service is important to the customer today, and if you want to get really out there with what we may see, what about a concierge service? At the moment, when we buy a new car we want it to drive well, if it breaks down we want to be able to call someone, if it gets serviced you want to be there for as little time as possible, or you want wireless so that you can work while you wait for your car to be serviced. . . . But you could take concierge to another level, like the American Express service and provide a series of exceptional value added services to customers. There are a segment of customers that will pay a bit more for such a service. (Australia, 2009)

Another respondent commented on how it can be beneficial to offer the same product at a different service level, charging a premium for better service, for instance:

> Some petroleum retailers are looking at dedicated premium lane, so when you drive in, you can choose to stop and fill it up yourself, or you can have someone come out to the car and fill it up for you and check your oil, wash your windscreen, tire pressure. . . . It doesn't matter how tough the economy is, there is a market for that stuff. It's about understanding the added value that you offer. (New Zealand, 2009)

The value added to the customer via enhanced service is profound, with customer loyalty and appreciation a given. At the same time, service can directly address individual needs for security, safety, and risk aversion, as can be seen in the provision of automotive services.

The very best retailers therefore stand apart by identifying and understanding customer insight, developing a range of retail offers that include the following:

1. Entertainment
2. Education
3. Local responses to global concerns
4. An integrated, multichannel environment
5. Product cocreation
6. Superior service

Part III Summary

In this part of the book we have taken a much more detailed look at the retail industry and how it has responded to facets of consumer resistance. It is clear that retailers need to think strategically and act ethically with a concern for the environment. The community is calling for more social responsibility on the part of retailers, both in their stores and throughout the supply chain. CSR is now an established part of business operations and it will continue to be well into the foreseeable future. CSR is a key requirement for a business wishing to be sustainable in the long term. As more governments move to introduce carbon-pricing and emissions-trading schemes, the retail industry will need to be responsive to their suppliers and to the community in fulfilling the requirements of this legislation.

In concluding part III, we call for the retail industry to lead via innovation, and we provide a range of examples of best practice in retail that work to minimize consumer resistance. It is clear that transparency of business operations and the need to educate and entertain the customer will remain important, and these consumer trends do, in fact, provide a range of competitive options for astute retailers.

CHAPTER 9

Conclusion

Throughout this book, we discuss the need for retailers to understand and learn more effective ways of managing inscrutable shoppers, and we believe this text provides an in-depth introduction to consumer resistance—a topic that requires further research and understanding as it directly applies to retailers. In understanding the inscrutable shopper, businesses are encouraged to review their value proposition and commit to scrutinizing their direct (within the organization) and indirect (on part of customers and suppliers) effects (which are often multidimensional) on society. For instance, a commitment to reduce waste can lead to cost efficiencies and increased market share due to an improved public image. Even the issue of waste is multidimensional, and therefore it is important to consider waste in economic, environmental, and social terms. Economic waste includes monetary aspects, such as the efficient allocation of financial resources. Environmental wastage can include consideration for renewable resources and reducing the organization's carbon footprint (emissions). Finally, social waste may include issues around urban planning and transport, local and individual lifestyles, and ethical consumption.

In this book, we detail consumer macro and micro shifts and in particular note that several mainstream movements, such as downshifting, are part of bigger shifts in values, attitudes, and the notion of what constitutes success for the consumer. A question arises: Are contemporary organizations willing and able to accommodate these movements? In some instances, we are seeing clear strategies to accommodate consumer movements, such as with regard to green marketing, which has turned the ecologically sustainable and ethical consumption practices of groups such as vegetarians into niche markets (as have voluntary simplicity and downshift movements). This is evidenced by the new commodity-laden magazine *Real Simple*. The challenge for retailers is to examine more closely the lived practices of these inscrutable shoppers and find ways to infuse their products and services into the cultural lifeblood of these people.

With this book we wanted to bring to life the notion that the inscrutable shopper is exerting concerted effort to minimize his or her personal, as well as organizational contribution to the environment. We detailed the notion of the *"waste-not mentality"* and discussed how consumption habits such as "do it yourself" and "find it yourself" are becoming increasingly common means to achieve this. The motivations underpinning such behaviors are economic, environmental, and social in nature, as well as emotional and aspirational, as consumers search for greater personal meaning and novelty from their shopping experiences. Although it can be argued that the economic conditions have increased this shift in consumer thinking and behavior, *the consumption behaviors that underpin the inscrutable shopper are not just a passing fad; rather, they (particularly the mainstream movements) are fast becoming an entrenched part of consumer culture.*

However, it is important to note that these movements and consumption (or avoidance) behaviors do not necessarily spell doom and gloom for retailers; rather there are several opportunities, as detailed in this book. For instance, the "do it yourself" consumption shifts present an interesting and lucrative opportunity to brands in that consumers are prepared (and to some degree expect) to offer their own intellectual property and effort, and provide ideas that feed directly into product conceptualizations, manufacture and distribution. Now widely termed "cocreation," this strategy not only allows consumers to design and potentially produce their own ideas (or designs), but also offers a deeper relationship to the product and brand via enhanced participation, affiliation, and ultimately, meaning. Skating brand *Vans* is one of many brands capitalizing on the concept of consumer cocreation. For Vans, social network sites enable consumers to build custom shoes online while chatting with friends in real time about the product design. Customers can click on a link ("Invite friends to design with you"), giving them the ability to access friends who can join and give a thumbs-up or thumbs-down on the design, as well as make suggestions. Katie Bongiovanni, Vans' director of e-commerce, reported sales and traffic increased: "It's preliminary, but the customers who have talked to us about it have been really happy with it," she said. "This is really how our consumer lives online right now. The collaborative part of it is resonating."[1]

What is important in this new world of increasingly proactive, demanding, skeptical, and cynical inscrutable shoppers is that there is a genuine need to be transparent. And transparency, like charity, starts in the home. Retailers need to work on their internal processes and procedures right down to the supply chain and even beyond the sale of their products and into consumption and disposal. The shift toward transparency requires a focus on the whole chain, including suppliers, affinity partners, customers, and investors. Consumer scrutiny also extends to every element of the product life cycle: its footprint, from how it was made and used to how it is disposed of. Business transparency is therefore more than a CSR policy, and it needs to extend beyond an individual brand or product to every element of business and stages of a product's life cycle.

As we have seen from the anti-advertising movement, consumers are increasingly skeptical of commercial messages, and they are turning to the collective wisdom and experience of their peers and social communities about products. The growth of the online channel as a research and information portal presents a challenge (and opportunity) for business, with increased transparency bringing scrutiny to an all-time high and people can more easily find out more about corporate environmental claims. Word-of-mouth is still perceived to be very credible, especially as consumers consider and try to comprehend complex product innovations. Websites, search engines, blogs, product ratings sites, podcasts, and other digital platforms have opened significant opportunities for tapping into consumers' social and communication networks to diffuse credible "word-of-mouse" about green products. Consumers are also fuelling the discussion through sites like Greenwashingindex.com, which allows them to upload and critique questionable ads, so organizations might as well join the conversation.

In essence, modern retailing requires that products and services (and retail brands) meet a high level of authenticity, as consumers are skeptical about the messages they receive and are ready to punish organizations when consumers' internal motivations are not aligned with their experience with the product, service, brand, or retailer.

The retail industry is so enmeshed in our social, economic, technological, political, and now environmental history that it can be difficult to tease out the issues important to the customer. This book, particularly part I, has provided the background and some interesting perspectives on why there is so much debate about the changes in many nations, particularly the emerging nations, about when and how retail should develop in their countries. Part I also introduced the concepts of the ethical, the green, and the activist as representing three of the major types of consumers who can be seen as inscrutable.

In part II, the book moved on to a more detailed discussion of consumer resistance by identifying macro- and micro-level trends and values that are then placed within a model of consumer resistance. The macro trends include nostalgia, cocooning, and enhanced social, cultural, and technological mobility. Internal motivations for consumer resistance are identified as economic value, health, convenience, identity creation, security, safety, and risk aversion, as well as empowerment through, collectives. The chapter concludes with a discussion of the issues relating to experience the consumer experience that are key for retailers: boredom, cynicism, too much choice, and potential conflict.

Research has indicated that consumers may be following trends that lead to consumer resistance. Trends such as voluntary simplification and downshifting are common. Consumers may be acting either individually by avoiding or minimizing contact with certain retailers, brands, or products, as they perceive that the engagement would result in a value conflict or unmet needs, or collectively, as we discussed many types of movements both mainstream and fringe, including the anti–chain store and antisweatshop movements.

Part III reminds the reader that CSR is a permanent feature of the business environment and that the consumer is very alert to business' attempts to short-circuit participation in efforts to reduce pollution in product manufacture and the supply chain, including distribution and waste reduction. All these responsibilities not only impose a considerable burden of communication and innovation on the industry but also provide many opportunities to improve profits via exploiting efficiencies in business operations that meet customers' calls for local providers of quality, decently priced merchandise.

Finally, the book reminds the reader that the inscrutable shopper is a savvy and educated individual who cannot be fooled by half-truths in advertising and business operations. The retailer who participates in green-washing is taking a huge risk, including provoking the wrath of a customer who does not appreciate, let alone quietly accept, false claims by a retailer wishing to position themselves as being more environmentally responsible than they actually are.

The contemporary retailer faces many challenges to meet the demands of the inscrutable shopper. Flexibility, innovation, differentiation, transparency, and a constant search for business-process improvements are part of the solution, as is the requirement to stay closely in touch with the customer through current and emerging advances in communication and technology. The inscrutable shopper is here to stay; the retailers who are responsive to this complex customer will maintain profitable businesses of the future.

Notes

Introduction

1. Kates and Belk (2001), p. 429.
2. Thompson (2004).
3. Kozinets and Handelman (1998).
4. Moisio and Askegaard (2002).
5. Laukkanen and Kiviniemi (2010).
6. Ho, Vermeer, and Zhao (2006).
7. Kleijnen, Lee, and Wetzels (2009).
8. Higginbottom D. (2011).
9. Lee, Fernandez, and Hyman (2009).
10. Schwartz (2004).
11. Schwartz (2004).
12. Humphrery (2009).
13. Kozinets and Handelman (2004).
14. Cherrier (2009).
15. Humphrery (2009).

Chapter 1

1. Marx (1990).
2. Baudrillard (1998).
3. Wood (2004).
4. Zola (1995).
5. Izberk-Bilgin (2010), p. 300.
6. Izberk-Bilgin (2010), p. 303.
7. Izberk-Bilgin[0] (2010), p. 307.
8. Chivers (2011).
9. Chivers (2011).

Chapter 2

1. Rappaport (2000), p. 162.
2. Rappaport (2000), p. 143.
3. Rappaport (2000).

4. Minahan and Beverland (2005), p. 30.
5. Chung (2001).
6. Huddleston, Schrader and Minahan (2010).
7. Kumar (2010).
8. McPhee and Fitzgerald (1987).
9. Switzer (2011).
10. Hine (2002).
11. Barletta (2003).
12. Minahan and Beverland (2005).
13. Schor (1999).
14. Schor (1999).

Chapter 3

1. Firat and Venkatesh (1995).
2. Baudrillard (1998).
3. Firat and Venkatesh (1995).
4. Gabriel and Lang (1995).
5. Freestone and McGoldrick (2008).
6. Harrison, Newholm, and Shaw (2005).
7. The Cooperative Bank (2010).
8. IGD (2010).
9. Harrison, Newholm, and Shaw (2005).
10. Roberts (1996).
11. Grande (2007).
12. Ethisphere (2011).
13. Organic Trade Association (2010).
14. The Telegraph (2010).
15. Cadilhon (2009).
16. Eckersley (2010).
17. Fair Trade Association (2010).
18. Datamonitor (2010).
19. Craig-Lees and Hill (2002).
20. Cherrier (2009).
21. The Co-Operative Bank (1999).
22. Fair Trade Association (2010).
23. Natural Marketing Institute (2010).
24. Fair Trade Association (2010).
25. CSR Wire (2010).
26. Mahoney (2008).
27. Moisander and Pesonen (2002).
28. Havas Media.

29. Harris Interactive.
30. The Shelton Group.
31. Carlsson, Garcia, and Löfgren (2010), p. 407.
32. Cherrier (2009), pp. 181–190.
33. Reverend Billy (2011).
34. McClish (2009).
35. Hindley (2009), pp. 118–126.

Chapter 4

1. Datamonitor (2007).
2. Fournier (1998).
3. Izberk-Bilgin (2010).
4. Minahan and Wolfram (2007), pp. 5–21.
5. Popcorn (1991).
6. Williams (2009).
7. Orlikowski (2007), pp. 1435–1448.
8. Trendwatching (2008).
9. Arai and Pedlar (2003).
10. Minahan and Wolfram Cox (2007); Campbell (2005).
11. Knitting Guild of America (2007).
12. Wei (2004).
13. Leggatt (2009).
14. O'Rourke (2011).
15. Fischer and Byron (1997), pp. 89–97.
16. India Retail Report (2010), pp. 7–9.
17. Raven (2004), pp. 198–214.
18. Gruber and Hungerman (2008), pp. 831–862.
19. Tilley (2010).
20. Organic Trade Association (2010).
21. Reimers and Clulow (2009), pp. 541–562.
22. Reimers and Clulow (2009), pp. 541–562.
23. Sands (2009).
24. Zumuda (2011).
25. Kim (2010), pp. 143–148.
26. Sands (2009).
27. Trendwatch.
28. Business Wire (2008).
29. Edelman (2007).
30. Ganim Barnes (2005), p. 1.
31. Odou and de Pechpeyrou (2010).
32. Nowell (2008).

33. Toffler (1970).
34. Schwartz (2004).
35. Iyengar and Lepper (2000), pp. 995–1006.

Chapter 5

 1. Cherrier (2008).
 2. Kozinets and Handelman (2004), pp. 691–704.
 3. Humphrey (2009).
 4. Fournier (1998), pp. 88–91.
 5. Cherrier (2009).
 6. Halliwell (2008).
 7. Halliwell (2008).
 8. See Campbell (1992).
 9. Campbell (2005), pp. 23–42.
10. Fight Club (1999).
11. Rivoli (2005).
12. Fournier (1998).
13. Craig-Lees and Hill (2002).
14. Cherrier (2009).
15. Cherrier (2009).
16. Woodward (2004).
17. Levy (2005), pp. 176–189.
18. Levy (2005), pp. 176–189.
19. Levy (2005), pp. 176–189.
20. Levy (2005), pp. 176–189.
21. Juniu (2000), p. 69.
22. Nelson, Paek, and Rademacher (2007), pp. 141–156.
23. Nelson, Paek, and Rademacher (2007), pp. 141–156.
24. Nelson, Paek, and Rademacher (2007), pp. 141–156.
25. Hamilton and Mail (2003).
26. Hamilton (2003).
27. Hamilton (2003).
28. Smith (2011).
29. Schor (1998), p. 113.
30. Hamilton and Mail (2003).
31. Shi (2001).
32. Taylor (2007).
33. Gardner (2009).
34. Fournier (1998).
35. Minahan and Beverland (2005), p. 98.
36. Minahan and Beverland (2005), p. 118.

37. Diana (2010).
38. Walmart: The High Cost of Low Price (2005).
39. Klein, Smith, and John (2004), p. 92.
40. Diana (2010).
41. Hartenstein (2010).
42. Fournier (1998).
43. Cherrier (2008).
44. Humphrey (2009).
45. Carducci (2006), pp. 116–138.
46. Stewart (2007).
47. LeVine (2005).
48. Rumbo (2002), pp. 127–148.
49. Kotler and Andreason (1991).
50. Rumbo (2002), pp. 127–148.
51. Harold (2004), pp. 189–211.
52. Reverend Billy and the Church of Life After Shopping (2011).
53. Reverend Billy and the Church of Life After Shopping (2011).
54. Jones (2004).
55. Klein (2000).
56. Harrison and Scorse (2004).
57. *Jane Doe et al v. Walmart Stores*, International Labor Rights Fund.
58. Scroop (2008b), pp. 947–968.
59. Scroop (2008a), pp. 925–949.
60. Verdant.net (2011).
61. Luddite (2010).
62. The Economist (2009).
63. Binfield (2004).
64. Weil and Rosen (1995), pp. 95–133.
65. Seligman (2002), pp. 114–116.

Chapter 6

1. Tomlinson and Evans (2005).
2. Orange (2010).
3. Daley (2010); Orange and Cohen (2010).
4. GMA and Deloitte (2009).
5. Mohan (2009).
6. Manget, Roche, and Münnich (2009).
7. EcoSecurities, ClimateBiz and Baker & McKensie (2009), pp. 4.
8. Corporate Sustainability and Responsibility International (2010).
9. Cone and The Boston College Center for Corporate Citizenship (2008).
10. TNS (2008).

11. Ottman, Stafford, and Hartman (2006), pp. 22–36.
12. Levitt (1960).
13. Environmental Affairs Council (2008).
14. Murray (2010).
15. Euromonitor (2008).

Chapter 7

1. Hartman (2009).
2. UNESCO (1997).
3. Nielsen and Thomsen (2007), p. 25.
4. GreenBiz (2009).
5. Greenbiz (2010).
6. Perruzzi (2008).
7. Marshall (2008).
8. Seifer (2006), pp. 51–52.
9. USGBC (2009).
10. USGBC (2009).
11. Simpson, Power, and Samson (2007), pp. 28–48.
12. Brody (2010).
13. Rao and Holt (2005).
14. IBM (2009), p. 22.
15. Reuters (2008).
16. FDF (2008).
17. Fair Trade Association Australian & New Zealand (2009).
18. Berry (2009).
19. Walmart (2007).
20. Mallett (2007).
21. SmartWay (2009).

Chapter 8

1. Bitner (1992); Lin (2004); Mattila and Wirtz (2001).
2. Harris, Harris, and Baron (2001).
3. Khaleejtimes (2010); Gerrity (2009); Community Times (2011).
4. Chain Store Age (1994).
5. Slade (2008).
6. Slade (2008).
7. Reimers (2010).
8. Arnold, Kozinets, and Handelman (2001).
9. Arnold, Kozinets, and Handelman (2001), p. 243.

10. Sands, (2009).
11. Stancu and Smith (2006).
12. PayPal (2008).
13. Rose, Hair, and Clark (2011).
14. Erick Schonfeld, (2010).
15. Rigby (2010).
16. Kozinets, Hemetsberger, and Schau (2008).
17. Small Business (2011).

Chapter 9

1. Zumuda (2009).

References

7-Eleven. (2008). 7-Eleven cites franchisee partnership as the key to being named 2008 Franchisor of the Year. Retrieved June 23, 2009, from http://www.7eleven.com.au/news/franchisor-of-the-year-2008.php

Anonymous. (2009, April 29). Finding the green in today's shoppers: Sustainability trends and new shopper insights. Retrieved October 12, 2010, from http://www.ahcgroup.com/mc_images/category/93/deloitte_on_competing_on_green_with_shoppers.pdf

Anonymous. (2009, December 23–28). To consume is to be human, for better or worse. *Australian Financial Review*, 62.

Anonymous. (2009, September). Social media advances the sustainability dialogue: New ways to powerfully engage stakeholders. *SDialogue*. Retrieved October 12, 2010, from http://sdialogue.com/publications/white-papers/social-media-advances-the-sustainability-dialogue

Anonymous. (2009). Company website statistics. Facebook.com. Retrieved June 20, 2009, from http://www.facebook.com/press/info.php?statistics

Anonymous. (2009). Environment suffers as global financial crisis concerns hits home. Mobium Group. Retrieved March 12, 2010, from http://www.mobium.com.au/pdf/Green-Tracker%20release%20120309.pdf

Anonymous. (2009). Facts and figures: Global Fairtrade in 2009. Fairtrade Australia and New Zealand. Retrieved February 10, 2009, from http://www.fta.org.au/about-fairtrade/facts-figures

Anonymous. (2009). U.K. retailers Tesco, Marks & Spencer report progress in reducing carbon emissions. GreenBiz. Retrieved June 8, 2010, from http://www.greenbiz.com/news/2009/06/08/uk-retailers-tesco-marks-spencer-report-progress-reducing-carbon-emissions

Anonymous. (2010, August 20). Thousands plot IKEA guerrilla game. *Inside Retailing Online*. Retrieved February 12, 2011, from http://www.insideretailing.com.au/Latest/tabid/53/ID/8921/Thousands-plot-Ikea-guerilla-game.aspx

Anonymous. (2010, September). *Environmental sustainability and the green customer*. Melbourne, Australia: Australian Centre for Retail Studies, Monash University.

Anonymous. (2010). 2010 Cone shared responsibility study, who's responsible? Retrieved August 22, 2010, from http://www.coneinc.com/news/request.php?id=3198

Anonymous. (2010). Climate confidence monitor 2010. HSBC. Retrieved February 10, 2010, from http://www.hsbc.com/1/PA_1_1_S5/content/assets/sustainability/101026_hsbc_climate_confidence_monitor_2010.pdf

Anonymous. (2010). Community report card 2010. *Bunnings Warehouse*. Retrieved November 20, 2010, from http://www.bunnings.com.au/resources.ashx/SystemRadControlAssets/547/Name/B491C6CD5D24769ACEA7DA0B2906AE30/Community_Report_Card_2010.pdf

Anonymous. (2010). Marks & Spencer's Plan A update highlights profits. GreenBiz. Retrieved June 10, 2010, from http://www.greenbiz.com/news/2010/06/10/marks-spencer-plan-a-update-highlights-profits-progress-going-green

Arai, S., & Pedlar, A. (2003). Moving beyond individualism in leisure theory: A critical analysis of concepts of community and social engagement. *Leisure studies (22)*, 1–18.

Arnold, S., Kozinets, R., & Handelman, J. (2001). Hometown ideology and retailer legitimation: The institutional semiotics of Wal-Mart flyers. *Journal of Retailing, 77* (2), 243–271.

Attracting. (2007). *Attracting and retaining a cross-generational workforce.* Melbourne, Australia: Monash University, Australian Centre for Retail Studies.

Barletta, M. (2003). *Marketing to women: How to understand, reach, and increase your share of the world's largest market segment.* Chicago, IL: Dearborn Trade Publishing.

Baudrillard, J. (1998). *The consumer society: Myths and structures.* London, UK: Sage.

Berry, B. (2009). Going green: The future of the retail food industry. *Agriculture and Agri-Food Canada.* Retrieved April 3, 2010, from http://www.ats.agr.gc.ca/amr/4531-eng.htm

BFA. (2008). Australian Organic Market Report 2008, Biological Farmers of Australia Co-op Ltd. Retrieved June 2, 2011, from http://www.bfa.com.au/Portals/0/BFAFiles/AOMR2008-Part1.pdf

Binfield, K. (2004). *Writings of the Luddites.* London, UK: Johns Hopkins University Press: UK.

Bitner, M. J. (1992). Servicescapes: The impact of physical surroundings on customers and employees. *Journal of Marketing, 54*(2), 69–82.

Brody, P. (2010). 12 steps to a greener, more sustainable electronics supply chain. IBM Executive Brief. Retrieved June 2, 2011, from http://www.scribd.com/doc/45517605/12-Steps-Green-Supply-Chain-Strategies-from-IBM

Business Wire. (2008). Technomic finds that consumers want more sandwich variety. Retrieved June 2, 2011, from http://www.businesswire.com/news/home/20080521005667/en/Technomic-Finds-Consumers-Sandwich-Variety

Cadilhon, J. (2009, May 26–28). The market for organic products in Asia-Pacific. *Food and Agricultural Organization for the United Nations.* Retrieved February 4, 2011, from http://www.fao.org/docs/eims/upload/261001/Cadilhon%202009%20China%20BioFach%20presentation.pdf

Campbell, C. (1992). The desire for the new: Its nature and social location as presented in theories of fashion and modern consumerism. In R. Silverstone & E. Hirsch (Eds.), *Consuming technologies: Media and information in domestic spaces* (pp. 48–64). London, UK: Routledge.

Campbell, C. (2005). The craft consumer culture, craft and consumption in a postmodern society. *Journal of Consumer Culture, 5*(1), 23–42.

Carducci, V. (2006). Culture jamming: A sociological perspective. *Journal of Consumer Culture, 6*(1), 116–138.

Carlsson, F., Garcia, J. H., and Löfgren, Å. (2010). Conformity and the demand for environmental goods, *Environmental and Resource Economics, 47*(3), 407–421.

Chain Store Age. (1994). That's entertainment: Fantasy theme designs woo shoppers. *Chain Store Age Executive With Shopping Center Age, 70*(8).

Cherrier, H. (2009). Anti-consumption discourses and consumer-resistant identities. *Journal of Business Research, 62*(2), 181–190.

Chivers, J. (2011). My year without clothes shopping. Retrieved February 6, 2011, from http://myyearwithoutclothesshopping.com

Chung, C. J. (2001). Ms. Consumer. In C. J. Chung, J. Inaba, R. Koolhas, & S. T. Leong (Eds.), *Harvard Design School guide to shopping* (pp. 505–525). New York, NY: Taschen.

Community Times. (2011). KidZania Cairo Egypt's First Edutainment Center. *Community Times.*

Cone. (2008). Americans misunderstand environmental marketing messages. Retrieved June 2, 2011, from http://www.coneinc.com/content1136

Cone and The Boston College Center for Corporate Citizenship. (2008). 2008 Green Gap Survey. Retrieved June 2, 2011, from http://www.coneinc.com/stuff/contentmgr/files/0/57bfa0d65ae70c7e1122a05a9d0d67e0/files/2008_green_gap_survey_fact_sheet.pdf

Corporate Sustainability and Responsibility International. (2010). CSR Research Digests, research report. Retrieved June 2, 2011, from http://www.csrinternational.org/briefings/csr-research-digests/

The Cooperative Bank. (2001–2010). The Ethical Consumerism Report 2010. Retrieved June 1, 2010, from http://www.goodwithmoney.co.uk/ethical-consumerism-report-2010

Craig-Lees, M., & Hill, C. (2002). Understanding voluntary simplifiers. *Psychology & Marketing, 19*(2), 187.

Datamonitor. (2007). How to create brand loyalty among today's consumers. Datamonitor. June 29.

Deloitte. (2009). Lifecycle Assessment: Where is it on your sustainability agenda? Retrieved June 2, 2011, from http://www.deloitte.com/assets/Dcom -UnitedStates/Local%20Assets/Documents/us_es_LifecycleAssessmet.pdf

Diana, M. (2010). Consumer Boycotts. Retrieved June 2, 2011, from http:// american-business.org/2359-consumer-boycotts.html

Downshifting. (2005, November 1). Downshifting: Quitting the rat race. *Human Resources Magazine*. Retrieved December 18, 2010, from http:// www.humanresourcesmagazine.com.au/articles/56/0C036F56.asp ?Type=60&Category=1223

Eckersley, N. (2010, May 27). Worldwide Fairtrade sales hit $5.4 billion. *Australian food news*. Retrieved June 8, 2011, from http://www.ausfoodnews .com.au/2010/05/27/worldwide-fairtrade-sales-hit-54-billion.html

The Economist. (2009, November 6). Rethinking the Luddites. *The Economist*. Retrieved December 18, 2010, from http://www.economist.com/blogs/ freeexchange/2009/11/rethinking_the_luddites

Eco Securities, ClimateBiz, and Baker & McKensie. (2009).The Carbon Management and Offsetting Trends Survey Results 2009. Retrieved June 2, 2011, from http://www.cdmgoldstandard.org/fileadmin/editors/ files/2_news/market_trends_and_forecasts/EcoSecurities_Carbon _Management_and_Offsetting_Survey_2009.pdf

Edelman, M. (2007). Merchandising to the trysumer. Retrieved December 3, 2009, from http://ezinearticles.com/?Merchandising-To-The-Trysumer&id =428088

Environmental Affairs Council. (2008). Whole Foods Market Ink's Misleading and Deceptive Environmental Marketing and Labeling Practices. Retrieved June 2, 2011, from http://www.enviroaffairscouncil.org/blog/files/eac_letter _complaint_exhibits.pdf

Ethisphere. (2011). World's Most Ethical List. Retrieved June 1, 2011, from http://ethisphere.com/2011-worlds-most-ethical-companies/

Euromonitor. (2008, March 13). The green (and variegated) customer. Euromonitor Strategy Briefing, Euromonitor International, London, UK.

Fair Trade Association Australia & New Zealand. (2009). Fairtrade in Australia and New Zealand. Retrieved June 2, 2011, from http://www.fta.org.au/ about-fairtrade/facts-figures.

FDF. (2008). Our Five-Fold Environmental Ambition: 2008 Progress Report. Food and Drink Federation. Retrieved June 2, 2011, from http://www.fdf .org.uk/publicgeneral/environment_progress_report_finalversion.pdf

Firat, A., & Venkatesh, A. (1995, December). Liberatory postmodernism and reenchantment of consumption, *Journal of Consumer Research 22*, December 239–267.

Fischer, W., & Byron, P. (1997). Buy Australian made. *Journal of Consumer Policy, 20*(1), 89–97.

Fournier, S. (1998). Consumer resistance: Societal motivations, consumer manifestations, and implications in the marketing domain. *Special Session Summary: Advances in Consumer Research, 25*, 88–91.

A framework. (2008, January). A framework for pro-environmental behaviours. UK Department for Environment, Food and Rural Affairs. Retrieved August 22, 2010, from http://www.defra.gov.uk/evidence/social/behaviour/documents/behaviours-jan08-report.pdf

Freestone, O., & McGoldrick, P. (2008). Motivations of the ethical consumer. *Journal of Business Ethics, 79*, 445–467.

Gabriel, Y., & Lang, T. (1995). *The unmanageable consumer*. London, UK: Sage.

Gandolfi, F. (2005). Downshifting: Quitting the rat race. Retrieved June 2, 2011, from http://www.humanresourcesmagazine.com.au/articles/56/0C036F56.asp?Type=60&Category=1223

Ganim Barnes, N. (2005). The restructuring of the retail business in the US: The fall of the shopping mall. *Business Forum, 27*(1), 4–7

Gardner, N. (2009, March/April). A manifesto for slow travel. *Hidden Europe magazine*, 25.

Gerrity, M. (2009, March 18). KidZania readies for opening at Dubai Mall: Offering role-play Edu-tainment for children. Real Estate Channel.

GMA-Deloitte. (2009). Finding the green in today's shoppers: Sustainability trends and new shopper insights. Retrieved June 2, 2011, from http://www.deloitte.com/assets/Dcom-Shared%20Assets/Documents/US_CP_GMADeloitteGreenShopperStudy_2009.pdf

Grande, C. (2007, February 20). Ethical consumption makes mark on branding. *Financial Times*. February 20, 2007. Retrieved February 3, 2011, from http://www.ft.com/cms/s/d54c45ec-c086-11db-995a-000b5df10621.html

GreenBiz. (2009). U.K. retailers Tesco, Marks & Spencer report progress in reducing carbon emissions. GreenBiz. Retrieved June 8, 2010, from http://www.greenbiz.com/news/2009/06/08/uk-retailers-tesco-marks-spencer-report-progress-reducing-carbon-emissions

Greenbiz. (2010). Marks & Spencer's Plan A Update Highlights Profits. GreenBiz. Retrieved June 10, 2010, from http://www.greenbiz.com/news/2010/06/10/marks-spencer-plan-a-update-highlights-profits-progress-going-green

Green gap. (2008). Green gap survey factsheet. Retrieved August 22, 2010, from http://www.coneinc.com/stuff/contentmgr/files/0/57bfa0d65ae70c7e1122a05a9d0d67e0/files/2008_green_gap_survey_fact_sheet.pdf

Greenwald, R. (Producer & Director). (2005). *Walmart: The High Cost of Low Price* [Video]. United States: Brave New Films.

Gruber, J., & Hungerman, D. (2008). The church vs. the mall: What happens when religion faces increased secular competition? *Quarterly Journal of Economics, 123*, pp. 831–862.

Halliwell, E. (2008). We love to hate big brands. Retrieved June 2, 2011, from http://www.dailytelegraph.com.au/news/sydney-nsw/we-love-to-hate-big -brands/story-e6freuzi-1111116303533

Hamilton, C. (2003, November). Downshifting in Britain: A sea-change in the pursuit of happiness (The Australia Institute Discussion Paper No. 58).

Hamilton, C., & Mail, E. (2003, January). Downshifting in Australia: A sea-change in the pursuit of happiness (The Australia Institute Discussion Paper No. 50).

Harold, C. (2004). Pranking rhetoric: "Culture jamming" as media activism. *Critical Studies in Media Communication, 21*(3), 189–211.

Harris, R., Harris, K., & Baron, S. (2003) Theatrical service experiences: Dramatic script development with employees. *International Journal of Service Industry Management 14* (2), 184–199.

Harrison, R., Newholm, T., & Shaw, D. (2005). *The ethical consumer*. London, UK: Sage.

Harrison, A., & Scorse, J. (2004, April). Moving up or moving out? Anti-sweatshop activists and labor market outcomes (NBER Working Paper No. 10492).

Hartenstein, M. (2010). USA: Target boycotted for donating $150,000 to MN right-wing Republican Tom Emmer's campaign for governor. *New York Daily News*. Retrieved June 2, 2011, from http://www.corpwatch.org/article .php?id=15613

Hartman Group. (2009). Sustainability: The Rise of Consumer Responsibility, research report, Retrieved June 2, 2011, from http://www.hartman-group .com/publications/view/81

Higginbottom, D. (2011). Boys boycott and girls follow. Retrieved March 8, 2011, from http://www.consumersentiments.com.au/boys-boycott-girls-follow

Hindley, J. (2010). Breaking the consumerist trance: The Reverend Billy and the Church of Stop Shopping. *Capitalism Nature Socialism, 21*(4), 118–126.

Hine, T. (2002). *I want that: How we all became shoppers*. New York, NY: HarperCollins.

Ho, P., Vermeer, E. B., & Zhao, J. H. (2006). Biotechnology and food safety in China: Consumers' acceptance or resistance? *Development & Change, 37*(1), 227–254.

Huddleston, P., Schrader, J., & Minahan, S. (2010). It's a family affair: Mothers, daughters and siblings' shopping experiences. Proceedings of the Australia and New Zealand Marketing Academy Conference, Christchurch, New Zealand.

Humphrey, K. (2009). *Excess: Anti-consumerism in the West.* Melbourne, Australia: Wiley.

IBM. (2009). The Smarter Supply Chain of the Future: Global Chief Supply Chain Officer Study. Retrieved June 2, 2011, from http://www.escinst.org/pdf/CSCO_study.pdf

IIyengar, S. S., & Lepper, M. (2000). When choice is demotivating: Can one desire too much of a good thing? *Journal of Personality and Social Psychology, 79*(6), 995–1006.

India Retail Report. (2010). Q4 2010. *Business Monitor International,* pp. 7–9.

Izberk-Bilgin, E. (2010). An interdisciplinary review of resistance to consumption: Some marketing interpretations and future research suggestions. *Consumption Markets and Culture, 13*(3), 299–323.

Jane Doe I, et al. v. Wal-Mart Stores, Inc. No. CV 05-7307 (C.D. Cal. Dec. 11, 2006).

Jones, T. (2004). Half of US Food Goes to Waste. Foodproductiondaily.com. Retrieved June 2, 2011, from http://www.foodproductiondaily.com/Supply-Chain/Half-of-US-food-goes-to-waste

Juniu, S. (2000). Downshifting: Regaining the essence of leisure. *Journal of Leisure Research, 32*(1), 69.

Kates, S., & Belk, R. (2001). The meaning of lesbians and gay pride day: Resistance through consumption and resistance to consumption. *Journal of Contemporary Ethnography, 30*(4), 429.

Khaleejtimes. (2010, January 21). KidZania celebrates foundation day at Dubai Mall. *Khaleejtimes.*

Kim, I. (2010) Consumers' rankings of risk-reduction strategies in e-shopping. *International Journal of Business Research, 10*(3), 143–148.

Kleijnen, M., Lee, N., & Wetzels, M. (2009). An exploration of consumer resistance to innovation and its antecedents. *Journal of Economic Psychology, 30*(3), 344–357.

Klein, J. G., Smith, N. C., & John, A. (2004). Why we boycott: Consumer motivations for boycott participation. *Journal of Marketing, 68*(3), 92–109.

Klein, N. (2000). *No logo: Taking aim at the brand bullies.* Toronto, Canada: Knopf.

Kotler, P., & Andreason, A. (1991). *Strategic marketing for nonprofit organizations* (4th ed.). Englewood Cliffs, NJ: Prentice-Hall.

Kozinets, A., & Handelman, J. (2001). Hometown Ideology and Retailer Legitimation: The Institutional Semiotics of Wal-Mart Flyers. *Journal of Retailing, 77*(2), 243–271.

Kozinets, R. V., & Handelman, J. (1998). Ensouling consumption: A ethnographic exploration of the meaning of boycotting behavior. *Advances in Consumer Research, 25*(1), 475–480.

Kozinets, R. V., & Handelman, J. M. (2004). Adversaries of consumption: Consumer movements, activism, and ideology. *Journal of Consumer Research, 31*, (3) 691–704.

Kumar, J. (2010, August 23–14). Busy moms to benefit from TESCO's drive through supermarket. *Top News Singapore*, 31.

Landor Associates. (2007). Research by WPP companies reveals UK consumers ripe for green business. Retrieved June 2, 2011, from http://www.wpp.com/wpp/press/press/default.htm?guid=%7B11a9cc6b-5f74-4efd-adb8-d1c9a703c73d%7D

Laukkanen, T., & Kiviniemi, V. (2010). The role of information in mobile banking resistance. *International Journal of Bank Marketing, 28*(5), 372–388.

Leggatt, H. (2009, May 27). Iconic luxury accessory brand boosts online presence. Biz Report. Retrieved November 12, 2009, from http://www.bizreport.com/2009/05/iconic_luxury_accessory_brand_boosts_online_presence.html

Lee, M., Fernandez, K., & Hyman, M. (2009). Anti-consumption: An overview and research agenda. *Journal of Business Research 62*(2), 145–147.

LeVine, M. (2005). *Why they don't hate us: Lifting the veil on the axis of evil.* Oxford, UK: Oneworld Publications.

Levitt, T. (1960, July–August). Marketing myopia. *Harvard business review 38,* (July–August), 24–47.

Levy, N. (2005). Downshifting and meaning in life. *Ratio, 18*(2), 176–189.

Lin, I. Y. (2004). Evaluating a servicescape: The effect of cognition and emotion. *International Journal of Hospitality Management, 23*(2), 163–178.

Luddite. (2010). In *Compact Oxford English dictionary*. Retrieved June 1, 2011, from http://www.AskOxford.com

Mahoney, S. (2008). Study: Boomers, not Gen Y, biggest green shoppers. *Marketing Daily*. Retrieved June 8, 2011, from http://www.mediapost.com/publications/?fa=Articles.showArticle&art_aid=90173

Mallett, T. (2007). Shipping: Six steps to achieving retail's holy green grail. RedPrairie. Retrieved June 2, 2011, from http://www.redprairie.co.uk/uploadedFiles/ResourceCenter/Resources/Whitepapers/WP_GreenShip.pdf?LangType=2057

Manget, J., Roche, C., & Münnich, F. (2009). Capturing the Green Advantage for Consumer Companies. BCG Perspectives. Retrieved June 2, 2011, from https://www.bcgperspectives.com/content/articles/capturing_green_advantage_for_consumer_companies/

Marshall, C. (2008). Developers adjusting to shifting retail landscape, *Oakland Business Review*. Retrieved March 27, from http://blog.mlive.com

Marx, K. (1990). *Capital, volume 1*. London, UK: Penguin.

Mattila, A. S., & Wirtz, J. (2001). Congruency of scent and music as a driver of in-store evaluations and behavior. *Journal of Retailing, 77*(2) 273–289.

McClish, C. L. (2009). Activism based in embarrassment: The anti-consumption spirituality of the Reverend Billy. *Liminalities: A Journal of Performance Studies, 5*(2), 1–20.

McPhee, C., & Fitzgerald, A. (1987). *The non-violent militant: Selected writing of Teresa Billington-Grieg*. New York, NY: Routledge.

Milchanm, A. (Producer), & Fincher, D. (Director). (1999). *Fight Club* [Motion picture]. United States: 20th Century Fox.

Minahan, S. M., & Beverland, M. (2005). *Why women shop: Secrets revealed*. Melbourne, Australia: Wiley.

Minahan, S., & Wolfram Cox, J. (2007). Stitch'n bitch: Cyberfeminism, a third place and the new materiality. *Journal of Material Culture, 12*(1), 5–21.

Minahan, S., & Wolfram Cox, J. (2007). The aesthetic turn in management. International Library of Essays on Management. Aldershot, UK: Ashgate.

Mohan, M. (2009). Consumer education is key to attracting green shoppers, report shows. Greener Package. Retrieved June 2, 2011, from http://www.greenerpackage.com/green_marketing/consumer_education_key_attracting_green_shoppers_report_shows.

Moisander, J., & Pesonen, S. (2002). Narratives of sustainable ways of living: Constructing the self and the other as a green consumer. *Management Decision, 40*(4), 329–342.

Moisio, R. J., & Askegaard, S. (2002). Fighting culture: Mobile phone consumption practices as a means of consumer resistance. *Asia Pacific Advances in Consumer Research, 5*(1), 24–29.

Murray, J. (2010). Eco cleaning products are greenwashing customers, *Which?* Warns. Business Green. Retrieved June 10, 2010, from http://www.businessgreen.com/bg/news/1802554/eco-cleaning-products-greenwashing-customers-which-warns

Natural Marketing Institute. (2010). The LOHAS Consumer Trends Database—2010. Retrieved June 8, 2011, from http://www.nmisolutions.com/lohasd_segment.html

Nelson, M. R., Paek, H.-J., & Rademacher, M. A. (2007). Downshifting consumer = upshifting citizen? An examination of a local freecycle community. *The Annals of the American Academy of Political and Social Science, 614*(1), 141–156.

New eBay research. (2008). New eBay research reveals more consumers plan to resell holiday gifts online this year than ever before. Retrieved January 14, 2009, from http://news.ebay.com/releasedetail.cfm?ReleaseID=355225

Nielsen, A. E., & Thomsen C. (2007). Reporting CSR: What and how to say it. *Corporate Communications: An International Journal, 12*(1), 25–40.

Nowell, P. (2008). Brand trust and consumer cynicism. *The Drum.* Retrieved June 2, 2011, from http://www.thedrum.co.uk/indepth/1643-brand-trust-and-consumer-cynicism/

Odou, P., & de Pechpeyrou, P. (2010). Cynical consumers at work: From resistance to anti- consumption. ICAR/NACRE 2010 Symposium, Marseille, France.

Orange, E. (2010). From eco-friendly to eco-intelligent: So-called "green" products are flooding the marketplace, but is this trend actually benefiting the environment? A business futurist shows why businesses, consumers, and the environment all come out on the losing end of deceptive labeling. *The Futurist.* Retrieved June 2, 2011, from http://www.allbusiness.com/marketing-advertising/market-groups-green-market/15061074-1.html

Orange, E., & Cohen, A. M. (2010, September–October). From eco-friendly to eco-intelligent. *The Futurist.* Retrieved October 12, 2010, from http://findarticles.com/p/articles/mi_go2133/is_201009/ai_n55066576

Organic Trade Association. (2010). Industry Statistics and Projected Growth. Retrieved June 2, 2011, from http://www.ota.com/organic/mt/business.html

Orlikowski, W. J. (2007). Sociomaterial practices: Exploring technology at work. *Organization Studies 28*(9): 1435–1448.

O'Rourke, K. (2011, January 26–February 1). Hoax: Facebook to close March 15, 2011. *The Journal.* Retrieved June 2, 2011, from http://smujournal.zzl.org/Jan%2026.pdf.

Ottman, J., Stafford, E., & Hartman, C. (2006). Avoiding green marketing myopia: Ways to improve consumer appeal for environmentally preferable products. *Environment, 48*, 22–36.

Our Green World. (2008, December). Our green world. Retrieved September 14, 2009, from http://www.tnsglobal.com/_assets/files/TNS_Market_Research_Our_Green_World.pdf

PayPal. (2008). PayPal reports some online sales categories up this Xmas *eCommerce Report, 15*(9). Retrieved June 2, 2011, from http://www.ecommercereport.com.au/story60.php.

Peñaloza, L., & Price, L. (1993). Consumer resistance: A conceptual overview. In L. McAlister & M. Rothschild (Eds.), *Advances in consumer research* (pp. 123–128). Provo, UT: Association for Consumer Research.

Perruzzi, D. (2008). Green design: Construction vs. Renovation. Buildings. Retrieved June 2, 2011, fromhttp://www.buildings.com/ArticleDetails/tabid/3321/ArticleID/5855/Default.aspx

Popcorn, F. (1991). *The Popcorn report: Faith Popcorn on the future of your company, your world, your life.* New York, NY: Doubleday.

Rao, P., & Holt, D. (2005). Do green supply chains lead to competitiveness and economic performance? *International Journal of Operations & Production Management, 25*(9), 898–916.

Rappaport, E. D. (2000). *Shopping for pleasure: Women in the making of London's West End.* Princeton, NJ: Princeton University Press.

Raven, P. (2004). An exploratory study on retail service quality, in Kuwait and Lebanon. *Journal of Services Marketing, 18*(3), 198–214.

Razorfish. (2008). The Razorfish consumer experience report. Retrieved June 5, 2009, from http://feed.razorfish.com/downloads/Razorfish_FEED08.pdf

Reimers, V. V. (2010). *Designing convenient retail centres: What it entails and why it's important.* Saarbrücken, Germany: Lambert Academic Publishing.

Reimers, V. J., & Clulow, V. G. (2009). Retail centres: It's time to make them convenient. *International Journal of Retail and Distribution Management, 37*(7), 541–562.

Reverend Billy. (2011). Reverend Billy and the Church of Life After Shopping. Retrieved June 1, 2011, from http://www.revbilly.com

Reuters. (2009, May 20). Twitter looks at ways to make money. WARC. Retrieved June 20, 2009, from http://www.warc.com/LatestNews/News/Twitter %20looks%20at%20ways%20to%20make%20money.news?ID=25157

Reuters. (2008). Wal-Mart to source more fruits and veggies locally. Reuters InterActive Carbon Markets Community. Retrieved June 2, 2011, from http://www.enn.com/business/article/37530

Reverend Billy and the Church of Life After Shopping. (2011). Retrieved January 20, 2011, from http://www.revbilly.com

Richardson, B., & Turley, D. (2006). Support your local team: Resistance, subculture, and the desire for distinction. *Advances in Consumer Research, 33*(1), 175–180.

Rigby, C. (2010). Asos to launch online marketplace. Internet Retailing. Retrieved June 2, 2011, from http://www.internetretailing.net/2010/05/asos-to-launch-online-marketplace/

Rivoli, P. (2005). *The travels of a T-shirt in the global economy: An economist examines the markets, power, and politics of world trade.* New York, NY: Wiley.

Roberts, J. A. (1996). Will the socially responsible consumer please step forward? *Business Horizons, 39*(1), 79–84.

Rose, S., Hair, N., & Clark, M. (2011). Online customer experience: A review of the business-to-consumer online purchase context. *International Journal of Management Reviews, 13*(1), 24–39.

Rumbo, J. (2002). Consumer resistance in a world of advertising clutter: The case of Adbusters. *Psychology & Marketing, 19*(2), 127–148.

Sands, S. (2009). Retail 2020: The future of retail in Australia and New Zealand. Australian Centre for Retail Studies, Monash University, Melbourne, Australia.

Schonfeld, E. (2010). Forrester forecast: Online retail sales will grow to $250 billion by 2014. TechCrunch. Retrieved June 2, 2011, from http://techcrunch.com/2010/03/08/forrester-forecast-online-retail-sales-will-grow-to-250-billion-by-2014/

Schor, J. (1998). *The overspent American: Why we want what we don't need*. New York, NY: Harper Perennial.

Schor, J. (1999, summer). The new politics of consumption: Why Americans want so much more than they need. *Boston Review*. Retrieved June 1, 2011, from http://bostonreview.net/BR24.3/schor.html

Schwartz, B. (2004). *The paradox of choice: Why more is less*. New York, NY: Harper Perennial.

Scroop, D. (2008a). The anti-chain store movement and the politics of consumption. *American Quarterly*, *60*(4) 925–949.

Scroop, D. (2008b). Local and national identities in the politics of consumption: The anti-chain store movement reconsidered. *History Compass, 6*(3), 947–968.

Seifer, B. (2006, August). Consumers and the future of green retail. *Environmental Design and Construction*, 51–52.

Seligman, D. (2002, December 23). The technophobes. *Forbes, 170*(13), 114–116.

Simpson, D., Power, D., & Samson, D. (2007). Greening the automotive supply chain: A relationship perspective. *International Journal of Operations & Production Management, 27*(1), 28–48.

Slade, M. (2008). Real Groovy—a company adapting to change. Retrieved June 8, 2011, from http://www.nzherald.co.nz/business/news/article.cfm?c_id=3&objectid=10486047

Shi, D. (2001). *The simple life*. Athens, GA: University of Georgia Press.

Small Business. (2011). Consumers boycott companies after poor service. Retrieved June 2, 2011, from http://www.smallbusiness.co.uk/channels/sales-and-marketing/news/1514763/consumers-boycott-companies-after-poor-service.thtml

SmartWay. (2009). December 2009 e-update. Retrieved June 2, 2011, from http://www.epa.gov/smartwaytransport/newsroom/documents/e-update-Award-09.pdf

Smith, T. (2011). International downshifting week. Retrieved June 7, 2011, from http://www.downshiftingweek.com/

Stancu, C., & Smith, A. (2006). Food miles: The international debate and implications for New Zealand exporters (Business and Sustainability Series: Briefing Paper 1).

Stewart, K. (2007). *Ordinary affects*. Durham, NC: Duke University Press.

Switzer, M. (2011). Retailers: Raise your game. *Choice Online*.

Taylor, K. (2007, August 8). *The year I saved the world*. New York, NY: The Sun.

The Age. (2010, March 23). Westpac one of the world's most ethical companies. *The Age*. Retrieved June 1, 2011, from http://www.theage.com.au/business/world-business/westpac-one-of-the-worlds-most-ethical-companies-20100323-qsbz.html

Tester, K. (1999). The moral malaise of McDonaldization: The values of vegetarianism. In B. Smart (Ed.), *Resisting McDonaldization* (pp. 207–221), London, UK: Sage.

The Telegraph. (2010, April 12). Organic sales slump as shoppers tighten their belts. *The Telegraph*. Retrieved June 1, 2011, from http://www.telegraph.co.uk/earth/agriculture/organic/7580316/Organic-sales-slump-as-shoppers-tighten-their-belts.html

Thomas, P. (2010). Grayling's Paul Thomas on why companies greenwash. Retrieved June 2, 2011, from http://www.greenwisebusiness.co.uk/news/graylings-paul-thomas-on-why-companies-greenwash-1455.aspx

Thompson, C. J. (2004). Marketplace mythology and discourses of power. *Journal of Consumer Research, 31*(1), 162–180.

Tilley, M. (2010). Consumers Use Over $3.5 Billion in Coupons, Drive 27% Increase in Redemption for 2009. Retrieved June 2, 2011, from http://www.newsamerica.com/ourcompany/Documents/Inmar%20Press%20Release.pdf

TNS. (2008). Our Green World. Retrieved June 2, 2011, from http://www.tnsglobal.com/_assets/files/TNS_Market_Research_Our_Green_World.pdf

Toffler, A. (1970). *Future shock*. New York, NY: Random House.

Tomlinson, H., & Evans, R. (2005). Tesco stocks up on inside knowledge of shoppers' lives. Retrieved June 2, 2011, from http://www.guardian.co.uk/business/2005/sep/20/freedomofinformation.supermarkets

UNESCO. (1997). Educating for a Sustainable Future: A Transdisciplinary Vision for Concerted Action. Retrieved June 2, 2011, from http://www.unesco.org/education/tlsf/TLSF/theme_a/mod01/uncom01t05s01.htm#i

USGBC. (2009). The USGBC's Education Program—V3. Retrieved June 2, 2011, from http://www.usgbcri.org/content/index.php?option=com_content&view=section&layout=blog&id=11&Itemid=69

Verdant.net. (2011). *Overcoming consumerism*. Retrieved June 7, 2011, from http://www.verdant.net/

Victorian Employers' Chamber of Commerce and Industry. (2009, December). *Victoria's business carbon footprint survey*. East Melbourne, Australia: Author.

Walmart. (2007). Walmart Truck Fleet Rolls Fuel Savings. Retrieved July 23, 2011, from http://www.walmartstores.com

Wajcman, J. (2004). *Technofeminism*. Polity Press, Cambridge: UK.

Wei, C. (2004). Formations of norms in blog community: Into the blogo-sphere: Rhetoric, community and culture of web logs. Retrieved June 7, 2011, from http://blog.lib.umn.edu/blogosphere/formation_of_norms.html

Weil, M. M., & Rosen, L. D. (1995). A study of technological sophistication and technophobia in university students from 23 countries. *Computers in Human Behavior, 11*(1), 95–133.

Williams, S. (2009, January 7). Top 10 consumer/brand predictions for 2009. Sterling Brands. Retrieved June 20, 2009, from http://www.sterlingbrands.com/strategy/thought.php?thought_id=43

Woodward, I. (2003). Divergent narratives in the imaging of the home amongst middle-class consumers—Aesthetics, comfort and the symbolic boundaries of self and home. *Journal of Sociology, 39*(4): 391–412.

Zola, É. (1995). *The ladies' paradise.* B. Nelson (Trans.). Oxford, UK: Oxford University Press.

Zumuda, N. (2011, February 14). Retailers on quest to rekindle the personal touch of a bygone era. *Advertising age.* Retrieved June 2, 2011, from http://adage.com/article/news/macy-s-sears-petsmart-food-lion-rekindle-personal-touch/148836/

Zwiebach, E. (2009, August 19). Customer education key in sustainability effort. Supermarket News, Retrieved December 10, 2010, from http://supermarketnews.com/news/sustainability_panel_0819/

Recommended Reading

Baron, D. P. (2002, December). Private politics and private policy: A theory of boycotts. (GSB Working Paper No. RP1766). Retrieved February 4, 2011, from http://ssrn.com/abstract=367261 or doi:10.2139/ssrn.367261

Berman, B., & Thelen, S. (2004). A guide to developing and managing a well-integrated multi-channel retail strategy. *International Journal of Retail & Distribution Management, 32*(3), 147–156.

Bernick, L., & Guth, J. (2010, March). Stocking the shelves with green. *Five Winds International*. Retrieved April 20, 2010, from http://www.greenbiz.com/sites/default/files/GreenBizReports-Retail3.pdf

Binfield, K. (2004). *Writings of the Luddites*. Baltimore, MD: Johns Hopkins University Press.

Browne, R. (2008, August 10). Being green is the new black. *Sydney Morning Herald*. Retrieved December 3, 2009, from http://www.smh.com.au/lifestyle/fashion/being-green-is-the-new-black-20090403-9ny6.html

Cadilhon, J. (2009, May 26–28). The market for organic products in Asia-Pacific. *Food and Agricultural Organization for the United Nations*. Retrieved February 4, 2011, from http://www.fao.org/docs/eims/upload/261001/Cadilhon%202009%20China%20BioFach%20presentation.pdf

Campbell, C. (1997). Shopping, pleasure, and the sex war. In P. Falk & C. Campbell (Eds.), *The shopping experience* (pp. 166–176). London, UK: Sage.

Cauchi, S., & Mangan, J. (2010, January 10). We're not as green as we seem (or would like to be seen). *The Age*. Retrieved April 20, 2010, from http://www.theage.com.au/national/were-not-as-green-as-we-seem-or-would-like-to-be-seen-20100109-m00x.html

Choueke, M. (2008, January 12). Tesco should let data be its saviour. *Precision Marketing, 20*(21), 7.

Costa, J. A. (1994). *Gender issues and consumer behavior*. Thousand Oaks, CA: Sage.

Daley, J. (2010, August). Green fallout. *Entrepreneur*. Retrieved October 12, 2010, from http://www.entrepreneur.com/magazine/entrepreneur/2010/august/207498.html

Delevingne, L. (2009, January 20). Surprising survivors: Corporate do-gooders. *Fortune*. Retrieved August 22, 2010, from http://money.cnn.com/2009/01/19/magazines/fortune/do_gooder.fortune/index.htm

Department of Sustainability and Environment. (2009). 2009 green light report. *Sustainability Victoria*. Retrieved October 12, 2010, from http://greenlightreport.sustainability.vic.gov.au/assets/pdf/Greenlight_Report.pdf

Dholakia, R. R. (1999). Going shopping: Key determinants of shopping behaviors and motivations. *International Journal of Retail & Distribution Management, 27*(4), 154–165.

Elborough, K., & Zosel, R. (2009, July). *Victorian businesses' climate change knowledge, attitudes and behaviours*. East Melbourne: Victorian Employers' Chamber of Commerce and Industry.

Environics. (1999). The millennium poll on corporate social responsibility: Executive briefing. Retrieved January 27, 2011, from http://www.ipsos-mori.com/researchpublications/researcharchive/poll.aspx?oItemId=1851

Ferre, J. (2009, August 14). Drastic drop in plastic bag use in UK. *Australian Food News*. Retrieved December 3, 2009, from http://www.ausfoodnews.com.au/2008/08/14/drastic-drop-in-plastic-bag-use-in-uk.html

Finisterra do Paço, A. M., Lino Barata Raposo, M., & Leal Filho, W. (2008). Identifying the green customer: A segmentation study. *Journal of Targeting, Measurement and Analysis for Marketing, 17*(1), 17–25.

Forum for the Future. (2008, September). Retail leadership: What are the hallmarks of a sustainable retail business? *Kingfisher*. Retrieved August 22, 2010, from http://www.forumforthefuture.org/files/RetailLeadership_0.pdf

Friedman, M. (1999). *Consumer boycotts: Effecting change through the marketplace and the media*. New York, NY: Routledge.

Glazer, A., Kanniainen, V., & Poutvaara, P. (2008, May). Firms' ethics, consumer boycotts, and signalling (Discussion paper series No. 3498). German Institute for the Study of Labor (Forschungsinstitut zur Zukunft der Arbeit).

Goff, B. G., Bellenger, D. N., & Stojack, C. (1994). Cues to consumer susceptibility to salesperson influence: Implications for adaptive retail selling. *Journal of Personal Selling & Sales Management, 14*(2), 25.

Grande, C. (2007, February 20). Ethical consumption makes mark on branding. *Financial Times*. Retrieved February 3, 2011, from http://www.ft.com/cms/s/d54c45ec-c086-11db-995a-000b5df10621.html

Higginbottom, D. (2011). Boys boycott and girls follow. Retrieved March 8, 2011, from http://www.consumersentiments.com.au/boys-boycott-girls-follow/

Horne, D. R., & Craddock, T. (2005). *The European guide to gift and stored value*. London, UK: Giftex.

Kabel, M. (2007, July 17). Wal-Mart truck fleet rolls fuel savings. *LA Times*. Retrieved September 28, 2009, from http://www.mercedcan.com/pdf/7-17-07_LATimes.pdf

Klein, N. (2000). *No logo*, Toronto, Canada: Random House.

Kozinets, R. V., Hemetsberger, A., & Schau, H. J. (2008). The wisdom of consumer crowds: Collective innovation in the age of networked marketing. *Journal of Macromarketing, 28*(4), 339–354.

Leonard, A. (2010). *The story of stuff.* New York, NY: Free Press.

Lightfoot, L. (2010, April 22). Workforce goes green: Companies want to recruit people with the right environmental CVs. *The Independent.* Retrieved January 4, 2011, from http://www.independent.co.uk/student/career-planning/getting-job/workforce-goes-green-companies-want-to-recruit-people-with-the-right-environmental-cvs-1950136.html

Luck, E., & Giyanti, A. (2009). *Green marketing communities and blogs: Mapping customer's attitudes for future sustainable marketing.* Melbourne, Australia: Monash University.

Mahoney, S. (2008, September 9). Study: Boomers, not Gen Y, biggest shoppers. *Marketing Daily.* Retrieved January 30, 2011, from http://www.mediapost.com/publications/?fa=Articles.showArticle&art_aid=90173

Malhotra, N., Hall, J., Shaw, M., & Oppenheim, P. (2002). *Marketing research: An applied orientation.* Frenchs Forest, Australia: Prentice Hall.

Marlow, L. (2007). LOHAS: What every green business needs to know about their market. The Green Directory. Retrieved August 22, 2010, from http://www.thegreendirectory.com.au/green-news-and-events/green-marketing/lohas-lifestyles-of-health-and-sustainability.html

McGrath, M. (1998). Dream on: Projections of an ideal servicescape. In J. F. Sherry (Ed.), *Servicescapes: The concept of place in contemporary markets* (pp. 439–453). Chicago, IL: NTC Business Books.

Moutinho, L., Davies, F., & Curry, B. (1996). The impact of gender on car buyer satisfaction and loyalty: A neural network analysis. *Journal of Retailing and Consumer Services, 3*(3), 135–144.

Ogden-Barnes, S., & Minahan, S. (2006). The greydollarfella: An endangered species or a market opportunity? *Business Horizons, 49*(4), 287–292.

Ogle, J. P., Hyllegard, K. H., & Dunbar, B. H. (2004). Predicting patronage behaviors in a sustainable retail environment. *Environment and Behavior, 36*(5), 717–741.

Olafson, E. (2001). Multichannel retailing clicks. *Chain Store Age, 77*(1), 88.

Otnes, C., & McGrath, M. A. (2001). Perceptions and realities in male shopping behavior. *Journal of Retailing, 77*(1), 111–137.

O'Loughlin, E. (2010, April 9). Boom time for sustainable fashion. *Ragtrader.*

Palmer, D. (2008, November 18). American consumers warming to private label. *Australian Food News.* Retrieved December 3, 2009, from http://www.ausfoodnews.com.au/2008/11/18/american-consumers-warming-to-private-label.html

Palmer, D. (2008, October 2). The green revolution: Are customers buying it? *Australian Food News.* Retrieved December 3, 2009, from http://www .ausfoodnews.com.au/2008/10/02/the-green-revolution-are-consumers-buy-ing-it.html

Palmer, D. (2009: May 21). Australian supermarkets strengthen private label push. *Australian Food News.* Retrieved December 3, 2009, from http://www .ausfoodnews.com.au/2009/05/21/australian-supermarkets-strengthen -private-label-push.html

Peattie, K., & Crane, A. (2005). Green marketing: Legend, myth, farce or proph-esy? *Qualitative Market Research: An International Journal, 8*(4), 357–370.

Rangaswamy, A., & Van Bruggen, G. (2005). Opportunities and challenges in multichannel marketing: An introduction to the special issue. *Journal of Inter-active Marketing, 19*(2), 5.

Razorfish. (2008). The Razorfish consumer experience report. Retrieved June 5, 2009, from http://feed.razorfish.com/downloads/Razorfish_FEED08.pdf

Reimers, V. V. (2010). *Designing convenient retail centres: What it entails and why it's important.* Saarbrücken, Germany: Lambert Academic Publishing.

Reuters. (2009, May 20). Twitter looks at ways to make money. WARC. Retrieved June 20, 2009, from http://www.warc.com/LatestNews/News/Twitter %20looks%20at%20ways%20to%20make%20money.news?ID=25157

Rivoli, P. (2005). *The travels of a T-shirt in the global economy: An economist exam-ines the markets, power, and politics of world trade.* New York, NY: Wiley.

Roux, D. (2007). Consumer resistance: Proposal for an integrative framework. *Recherche et Applications en Marketing, 22*(4), 60–79.

Schelling, T. C. (2006). *Strategies of commitment and other essays.* Cambridge, MA: Harvard University Press.

Shao, C. Y., Baker, J. A., & Wagner, J. (2004). The effects of appropriateness of service contact personnel dress on customer expectations of service quality and purchase intention: The moderating influences of involvement and gen-der. *Journal of Business Research, 57*(10), 1164–1176.

Sherman, E., Schiffman, L. G., & Mathur, A. (2001). The influence of gender on the new-age elderly's consumption orientation. *Psychology & Marketing, 18*(10), 1073–1089.

Shields, R. (2008, December 28). The last word in disposable fashion. *The Inde-pendent.* Retrieved December 3, 2009, from http://www.independent.co.uk/ life-style/fashion/news/the-last-word-in-disposable-fashion-1213847.html

Strasser, S. (1999). *Waste and want: A social history of trash.* New York, NY: Met-ropolitan Books.

Strong, C. (1996). Features contributing to the growth of ethical consumerism: A preliminary investigation. *Marketing Intelligence & Planning, 14*(5), 5–13.

Thompson, C. J., & Hirschman, C. (1995). Understanding the socialized body: A post structuralist analysis of consumers' self-conceptions, body images and self-care practices. *Journal of Consumer Research, 28*(4), 550–571.

Tingley, J., & Robert, L. (2000). *Gendersell: How to sell to the opposite sex.* New York, NY: Touchstone Books.

Trendwatching. (2007, March). Trysumers. *Trendwatching.* Retreived July 14, 2009, from http://trendwatching.com/trends/trysumers.htm

Trendwatching. (2008, February). The expectation economy. *Trendwatching.* Retrieved July 14, 2009, from http://trendwatching.com/trends/expectationeconomy.htm

Turley, L. W., & Milliman, R. E. (2000). Atmospheric effects on shopping behavior: A review of the experimental evidence. *Journal of Business Research, 49*(2), 193–211.

Underhill, P. (2000). *Why we buy: The science of shopping.* New York, NY: Simon & Schuster.

Waldfogel, J. (2005). Does consumer irrationality trump consumer sovereignty. *The Review of Economics and Statistics, 87*(4), 691–696.

Zohar, A., & Morgan, G. (1996). Refining our understanding of hyper competition and hyper turbulence. *Organization Science, 7*(4), 460–464.

Index

Announcing the Business Expert Press Digital Library

Concise E-books Business Students Need for Classroom and Research

This book can also be purchased in an e-book collection by your library as

- a one-time purchase,
- that is owned forever,
- allows for simultaneous readers,
- has no restrictions on printing, and
- can be downloaded as PDFs from within the library community.

Our digital library collections are a great solution to beat the rising cost of textbooks. e-books can be loaded into their course management systems or onto students' e-book readers.

The **Business Expert Press** digital libraries are very affordable, with no obligation to buy in future years.

For more information, please visit **www.businessexpertpress.com/librarians**. To set up a trial in the United States, please contact **Sheri Allen** at *sheri.allen@globalepress.com*; for all other regions, contact **Nicole Lee** at *nicole.lee@igroupnet.com*.

OTHER TITLES IN OUR CONSUMER BEHAVIOR COLLECTION

Series Editor: **Naresh Malhotra**, *Georgia Institute of Technology*

Consumer Behavior: Women and Shopping by Patricia Huddleston and Stella Minahan
Store Design by Claus Ebster and Marion Garaus

www.ingramcontent.com/pod-product-compliance
Lightning Source LLC
Chambersburg PA
CBHW071840200326
41519CB00016B/4187